GODS, HEROES & MONSTERS

GODS, HEROES & MONSTERS

Myths & Legends from Around the World

Mark Daniels

Michael O'Mara Books Limited

First published in Great Britain in 2023 by
Michael O'Mara Books Limited
9 Lion Yard
Tremadoc Road
London SW4 7NQ

A CIP catalogue record for this book is available from the British
Library.

This product is made of material from well-managed, FSC®-certified
forests and other controlled sources. The manufacturing processes
conform to the environmental regulations of the country of origin.

ISBN: 978-1-78929-554-2 in hardback print format
ISBN: 978-1-78929-555-9 in ebook format

1 2 3 4 5 6 7 8 9 10

Cover illustrations by Bailey Sullivan
Jacket design by Natasha Le Coultre
Inside illustrations by Aubrey Smith
Designed and typeset by Claire Cater

Printed and bound by CPI Group (UK) Ltd, Croydon, CR0 4YY

www.mombooks.com

CONTENTS

INTRODUCTION

The story is one of the basic tools invented by
the mind of man, for the purpose of gaining
understanding. There have been great societies
that did not use the wheel, but there have been
no societies that did not tell stories.

Ursula Le Guin

our long-distant ancestors are sitting around
the campfire.

They have many unanswered questions.

At night, the stars scatter boundless maps
across the heavens, and the moon shapeshifts its course
through the darkness. And they ask: *What is that?* Each
day, they see the blaze of the burning sun climb high into
the sky and descend slowly beyond the horizon, and they
wonder: *Where does that go?* The seasons change. They
endure natural disasters. They experience love, pain, birth,
death, war, famine and Mondays. Endless impenetrable
questions kindle their curiosity and stir their imaginations.

Who are we, and where did we come from?

What happens when we die?

Across the world and across the generations, thousands
of campfires flicker in the darkness. As your ancestors

gather round the comfort of the embers, they start to share stories. They compose fantastical tales to explain the world and sky and sea and life that they see around them. Tales of magical creatures, towering beasts, guiding gods and vengeful deities. They weave legends of heroes and heroines, and of the underworld and the heavens.

All to create a narrative for the inexplicable.

Across thousands of years, the myths are passed from one person to another and on to the next, in every civilization across the world, many of them long before the art of writing has even been invented. Those very same myths continue to be shared today. They continue to inspire customs, storybooks and movies. From those ancient ancestors straight to your local cinema screen.

In this book, I continue in the tradition of our forefathers and foremothers, and recount the legends that they first imagined. Take your own epic voyage from the familiar myths of the Greeks, Romans and Egyptians, to the enchanting tales of the Native Americas, Australia's First Nations, West Africa, China, Japan and beyond.

For some myths, such as those from the Ancient Greeks, Romans, Indians and Babylonians, I retell the stories directly translated from original texts that are thousands of years old. Those stories that were etched in stone several millennia ago are directly rendered in these pages. In other civilizations, such as those in West Africa, Aboriginal Australia and Native America, their myths were not written down for dozens of generations, or were finally committed to paper by Western colonizers, who transposed their own beliefs onto the legends they were told. Some mythologies were deliberately and systematically oppressed, outlawed and even destroyed. In these cases, I continue in the oral tradition of humankind's ancestors in passing stories from one person to the other, and I narrate a version woven from the diverse tapestry of folklore.

You will hear tales from across the world and from across the history of humanity, categorized under the big questions those stories sought to answer. You'll hear the similarities and contrasts between different civilizations' myths of the world's first morning. You'll hear the legends of what will happen at the end of the world, then about the afterlife, then about love and war, about stars and storms, about heroines and gods.

So, take your place at the campfire that has been glowing since your ancient ancestors' first myth was told, and listen to their tales. Take your part in the continuous chain of storytellers and story listeners that stretches simultaneously backwards and into the future as far as humanity can reach.

Chapter 1
The Beginning and End of the World

erhaps one of the very first questions that our ancestors across the globe sought to answer was an existential one: *Where did we come from?*

It is a curiosity that has given rise to countless myths and inspired religions around the world. The legends about what might have happened on earth's first dawn are as diverse and numerous as the civilizations and communities who conceived them. From the life-giving mollusc and soil of the Yoruba people in West Africa, to the Rainbow Serpent of many of Australia's First Nations, to the debate between the gods of grain and cattle that the Ancient Mesopotamians retold, no two stories are quite the same.

What is remarkable, however, is the fact that there are nonetheless many correlations between origin myths told by different civilizations that were separated by oceans and several thousand years. There is no conceivable way that their legends could have influenced one another, and yet miraculous similarities do exist in different societies' telling of the dawn of time.

The parallels can be heard in the order in which the world came into existence. In the beginning, there was nothing. The world was in a dark, chaotic void with no life. The sky and the earth separated, and the very first light shone between them. From there, the barren land was filled with rivers, lakes and vast oceans, which in turn brought grass, trees and fruit. Next came the animals and beasts, and finally humanity was given life.

The exact details vary between civilizations, but the same general sequence of events can be heard in the creation myths of the Ancient Egyptians in 3000 BC, of the Ancient Greeks as early as 1800 BC, of the Jewish and Christian book of Genesis from about 500 BC, of the Incas in Peru in the AD 1200s, of the Māori people in New Zealand also in the AD 1200s, of the Sioux people of Native America around AD 1300, and several others besides.

Many belief systems speak of the beginning of time starting with nothing, from which earth and sky are among the very first basic elements to appear. After this often comes the creation of water, vegetation and animals, as well as deities representing particular fundamentals important to each civilization. Entirely unrelated mythologies have a Father Sky and a Mother Earth, a male sun and female moon, a god of chaos and one bringing order. One god is responsible for the creation of humankind, often moulded from clay or mud, and gives us clothes, the ability to make fire, and teaches us laws, morals and commandments. The Mayans, Greeks, Babylonians, Christians and others tell of having a second go at creating humanity when the first lot contravene those societal rules, often using a mighty flood to get rid of the lawless.

I suppose that when any of us have become philosophical and stripped the world back piece by piece to understand what was there at the beginning of it all, we have eventually been left with nothing but the land and the huge vault of the sky above it – from which all other things must come.

Likewise, there is a commonality among divergent mythologies about eschatology – a term for the end of times. If the universe has come from nothing, humanity has theorized that it must return to nothing. Unfortunately for us all, the end of the world tends to be much a more violent and terrifying event than its birth. The Ancient Indian story of the *Bhagavad Gita* (see Chapter 8), the Abrahamic religions of Judaism, Christianity and Islam, and the Norse concept of Ragnarök (see below) are among the belief systems to foresee a destructive apocalypse, after which the final judgement will be made on humankind. As we delve into some of these stories, delight in their variety and be amazed by their similarities.

RAGNARÖK
NORSE

Norse mythology originates from Scandinavia and Iceland in northern Europe, and you possibly know more of their gods than you may think. Their legends were passed from one generation to the next for many hundreds of years, before being committed to writing from about the thirteenth century AD onwards. The

Norse people had been making themselves very well acquainted across northern Europe and western Russia since the eighth century with their Viking invasions, as a result of which their mythology spread beyond their own borders. The Norse religion had a complex and colourful cast of gods and spirits as rich as that of the Greeks and Romans. The gods were each similarly dedicated to many different important aspects of life, and indeed there are many cognate deities between the Classical and the Norse civilizations.

As the father of the gods, Odin sits on his throne in Asgard with two ravens and two wolves acting as protectors and messengers. He is the god of war, as well as of wisdom and poetry, and has strong links to the dead and the slain. The universe is anchored in an ancient ash tree known as Yggdrasil, with its roots in the lower realms of the Underworld, and its branches reaching up to the heavens in the upper realms. The Midgard, or Middle-earth, is the realm of humans.

The Norse creation myth comes hand in hand with their concept of Ragnarök – the ultimate destruction of the world, in which fire, monsters and war obliterate the universe. The apocalypse is brought about because of the wayward nature of humanity and because of the warring between the gods. However, this annihilation soon reveals itself to be nothing other than a new beginning: the world is reborn, fresh, peaceful and sin-free. The story you'll hear in this chapter is taken from the thirteenth-century poem known as *Völuspà*, or *The Prophecy of the Seer*, one of several mythological poems in an Icelandic collection of texts of unknown authorship.

One of the most notable influences of Norse mythology is found in the English names for the days of the week. Monday and Sunday were named after the moon and sun respectively, with Tuesday to Friday dedicated to a different Norse god. It was in fact the Romans who first named the days of the week after the sun, the moon and five deities: Mars, Mercury, Jupiter, Venus and Saturn. You can still hear the remnants of those Roman names in the Spanish and French days of the week. The Nordics, however, took those Roman names for each day and simply switched their own corresponding god onto each one. The day named after the Roman god of war Mars changed names to the Norse god of war Tyr. It is the Norse versions that seem to have stuck in the Germanic languages, including English.

DAY	OLD NORSE	DEDICATED TO
Monday	Mánadagr	The moon
Tuesday	Týsdagr	Tyr, god of justice and war
Wednesday	Óðinsdagr	Odin, god of war, wisdom and poetry
Thursday	Þórsdagr	Thor, god of protection and thunder
Friday	Frjádagr	Freyja, goddess of love
Saturday	Laugardagr	Saturn, god of harvest
Sunday	Sunnudagr	The sun

IN THE BEGINNING, THERE IS NOTHING

At the very beginning of time, lives ancient ancestor Ymir, father of all the gods and spirits. There is no earth or land, no heavens above or salty waves below, and no green vegetation. Into this vast void, Odin and his brothers lift up Middle-earth, the human realm, and the sun shines brightly onto the drying land from the south. Grassland, trees and greenery fill the fertile earth.

The nine realms of the universe sit upon the mighty Yggdrasil tree. The realms of the gods and heavens above, Middle-earth for the humans, and the Underworlds below. It collects dew on its high branches that sustains the life below. On that first shore of Middle-earth, the gods find the first man and first woman: Ask and Embla. They have no breath, no soul, no hair, no voice, no colour in their face. Their fate seems doomed until three gods come together to create life: Odin breathes life into them, Hønir gives them movement, and Loki gives them hair and a healthy complexion.

A TERRIBLE PROPHECY IS MADE

All the gods gather together in the heavens, as a skilled seer of the future addresses king of the sky, Odin. 'I foresee a great hall, far from the sun,' she tells the mighty god. 'It is the dark home of Loki's daughter Hel, ruler of the dead. Poisonous venom drips down its walls and chimneys, as thick serpents coil around its walls.

'Wading through fast-flowing currents, I see dangerous men, murderers and adulterers. There, a dragon sucks on the blood of the dead and the monstrous wolf Fenrir tears their bodies asunder. Do you dare hear more?'

Odin nods solemnly, and the seer continues her grim prophecy. 'With the wolf Fenrir feeding on the flesh of the fallen, the home of the gods reddens with gruesome gore. After this, the sun grows dark even in summer and mighty storms begin to circle. Brothers battle each other to a bloody end, and cousins betray their family bonds as they lift swords against one another. The world becomes a terrible place, foul with seduction and adultery and all social order falls aside. Axes clash and swords flash, and no man will spare his neighbour.'

THE END OF DAYS

'While spirits dance, the watchman of the gods lifts up his sonorous horn and the sound reverberates across the world.' The seer looks Odin directly in the eyes as she speaks. 'Everyone in Hel's land of the dead quakes with fear as the ancient Yggdrasil tree – the very foundation of the universe – groans in its roots in the Underworld, and shakes in its rustling leaves in the heavens. And Odin, I see you frantic that Fenrir's blood-soaked jaws will come for you next.

'What will happen to the gods?' the seer continues.

'What will become of the elves and the dwarves? Garm, the bloodthirsty guard dog of the gates of Hel, howls terribly and breaks free of his chains. And now I see the terrifying fate of the gods. From the east, you are attacked by the deadly Hrym, heaving up his shield before him. A giant serpent churns up the frothing sea as it twists over the waves, and an eagle shrieks and tears strips from the bodies of men. From the north, Loki steers a boat through the fierce ocean currents; behind him follow the savage wolf Fenrir and an army of dreadful monsters of the giants.

'From the south, comes the fire god Surt, his sword shimmering as bright as the sun. Mountains fall, countless men are Hel-bound, and the heavens are split in two. And now I see you, Odin, stepping out to fight with the ferocious wolf Fenrir, and stepping out to fight Surt is god of the elves, Freyr. Here, you meet your tragic end, Odin. Your dear son flies forwards to avenge your death, and sinks his sword deep into the wolf's heart.'

A NEW BEGINNING

The seer's prophecy continues as she addresses all of the gods now: 'The sun turns black in the sky, the earth sinks into the sea, and the flickering stars shoot down from the eternal night. Flames engulf the whole world and the blaze reaches up to the very heavens. The howling of Hel's guard dog seals your fate.

'But now there's something new that I see.' The seer pauses and closes her eyes. 'The earth is new again. It rises from the sea, bright green and lush. Waterfalls tumble from the land and eagles hunt fish from high rivers. You gods do meet again – I can see it now. You gather and talk about the mighty past, remembering the ancient runestones of the great Odin. In verdant meadows, you will meet again.

'Where there is no life, new crops spring forth. Odin, your son returns from death to take his seat in your hall. I see that hall now, shimmering brighter than the sun, thatched with gold, and that's where all the gods will live eternally in peace. The ferocious dragon that sucks the blood from naked corpses flies over you now, and sinks out of sight forever.'

POPOL VUH
MAYAN

The K'iche' Mayans are one of the Maya peoples, who originally inhabited areas in Central America now known as Guatemala, Mexico, Belize and El Salvador. Their culture flourished particularly in the period from about AD 950 up to the protracted Spanish invasion and colonization in the early sixteenth century AD, when their history, language, religion and myths were systematically suppressed and outlawed. Their own written histories were burnt. You'll hear from many displaced cultures and peoples in this book, for whom their myths and legends remained the singular connection to their past. People for whom retelling the stories their grandparents had passed on to them became one of the only ways to keep a cultural identity alive. And so it was with the Mayans.

Popol Vuh is the K'iche' people's *Book of the Community*, and the version that exists today was committed to writing by a Spanish priest in 1701 from verbal retellings by the Mayans he met. It is these transliterations that inspire the creation story in this chapter. The original Mayan texts, complete with illustrations and a sophisticated hieroglyphic script, are no more. With the dismantling of the Mayan culture, the written account from 1701 is as much a historical record as it is a mythological tale. The outcome of this creation myth is that the gods seem to produce only male humans as the ancestors to all humankind. As with many ancient tales, it takes somewhat of a male-centric viewpoint but I have kept as close as possible to the original translation.

It is a story of the K'iche' people's place in the universe, rich with ancestral deities who passed down the lessons, morals and religion to their community. It is a place in the universe that was nearly taken away from them. And yet, through the centuries and generations of K'iche' people, their stories have survived and the voices of their ancestors have been given life once more.

IN THE BEGINNING, THERE IS NOTHING

Everything is silent. The boundless arc of the sky whispers with emptiness. There is not yet a single person, animal, bird, fish, crab, tree, rock, valley, meadow or forest. The broad sea alone rests beneath the vast void of the heavens.

Anything that might exist simply is not there. There is no earth, just the tranquil water alone murmurs in the eternal darkness.

And then a brilliant light emanates. The Maker, the Modeller, the Bearer and the Begetter are there in the water with the Sovereign Plumed Serpent, all dressed in turquoise feathers; these great wise ancestors, with all our knowledge. With their presence, the sky forms clearly now, and the great Heart of Sky, the thunderbolt god known as Huracan, emerges into existence.

AN AGREEMENT TO CREATE THE WORLD

Heart of Sky is the first to utter a word. He speaks with the Serpent and those first creation gods, as they deliberate the first dawn to mark the genesis of the world. In that dim light, they discuss how humankind will be born, how they will create the trees and vegetation, then how all living beings will be brought forth by Heart of Sky. It is agreed between the gods: 'Let us take the water away, and level out the flat land of the earth. Let the sky and the earth be separated.'

By their uttering these words, the world begins to form, with the land, sea and sky shaping separately. Then the gods call out for the mountains to rise up from the depths of the ocean, and the rivers and valleys to fall down their sides. Heart of Earth now stretches the canyons and rivers across the land, and through the gods' divine invocations, pine forests and cypress groves now rise from the rich soil to cover the whole earth.

THE CREATION OF ANIMALS

Then the gods fill the land with animals. The mountains and the forests are filled with the deer, birds, the puma, the jaguar, the serpent, the rattlesnake and the viper. The divine Grandmother and Grandfather of all beings, Xmucane and Xpiyacoc, give each animal its rightful place to live in harmony with the others: 'You deer will sleep along the rushing rivers and in the deep valleys. Here you can leap across the meadows and in the orchards, and you will rear your offspring in the forests.'

The birds are given their rightful space: 'You birds will make your home in the treetops and in the bushes. You will have space to multiply and bring up your offspring among all the branches of the trees.'

But something isn't right. The gods have no worship and no reverence for their creation of the world. 'Speak!' they demand of the world's animals. 'Speak to each other! Speak, each of you, to those of your own kind. Stop squawking and shrieking – actually speak out. Worship us and respect us! We are your Grandmother and Grandfather and together with Heart of Sky, Heart of Earth, the Sovereign Plumed Serpent and the others, we've made all of this for you. Worship us!'

But the gods are met with nothing but a cacophony of bleating and hooting. Each beast cries out in its own way, and nothing is recognizable. The creation gods have had enough. 'You can't even utter our divine names,' they tell the clueless creatures. 'We will have to replace you with something that can pay respect to us and our creation. So, you animals will have to make your habitats in the forests and the valleys. We'll create a different type of being who can worship us properly, and you will simply have to be the meat that sustains them.' This is why humans alone have the ability to speak.

MAKING THE MUD MAN

The gods gather together once more. 'Clearly, that first attempt wasn't good enough,' they agree. 'If we are to be remembered on earth, we need a being that can speak and that can worship us and honour us.' The gods form the first man from mud. He speaks, but isn't very bright. The mud is either too hard for him to move and turn his head, or it becomes sludgy and dissolves in the rain.

The Maker and the Modeller speak: 'We're doing this wrong again. If the mud hardens, these people can't move and they won't be able to multiply. Let us ask the divine Grandmother and Grandfather for a better version.'

MAKING THE WOODEN FIGURES

Heart of Sky addresses the gods: 'We need something that can speak and multiply. We are sustained by their words, their worship and their reverence. That is the only way we can be remembered on earth. I call upon you makers and shapers, creators and begetters, you moulders and woodworkers, ancestors of all creatures: run your hands over the corn and over the coral tree and use your mastery to carve out the mouth and face of the humans that will sustain us and provide for us.'

The divine Grandmother and Grandfather, Xmucane and Xpiyacoc, agree with all the creators that these wooden figures must be brought into existence. And at first, they are a successful creation. They look like people and they can speak well, and soon the population spreads across all the land of the earth. They multiply with sons, daughters, and new generations continue to thrive. But still, something isn't quite right. This lot can speak, but they've forgotten the gods that created them. They crawl on their hands and knees and remember nothing of Heart of Sky or the great Serpent that helped form the world. They are merely an attempt at making humanity, rather than being the real thing: no flesh on their frames, no blood coursing through their veins. Once again, the gods realize their mistakes.

A GREAT FLOOD

Heart of Sky rains down a terrible deluge from the heavens. Mankind, carved from coral tree, is smashed and ground into nothing, and womankind, fashioned from reeds, is crushed. The ancestral gods gouge out the eyes of this unholy population, since they don't even recognize their own creator. They cut off their heads, smash their bones and tendons, and the Crouching Jaguar eats their remains.

The earth falls into a darkness as black rain showers down. The wild animals descend on the villages of the wooden people. The creatures that the wooden people consumed, together with the dogs they refused to feed, enter their homes. The few people that remain try to escape. They climb the trees, but the vegetation refuses to support them; they pull themselves up to the roofs of their homes, but the stones crumble beneath them and crush their former inhabitants. The earth and the wooden people's very possessions turn against them. In fact, the more they own, the more there is to crush their thankless mouths and faithless faces.

This was no humankind, but a poor attempt at creating humankind. It is said that the spider monkey is the descendant of this imitation of man. They appear similar to humans, but they have no recollection of the gods that created them, nor any ability to worship or pay respect to the Heart of Sky.

THE CREATION OF HUMANITY

The sun, moon and stars haven't formed yet, but the first dawn is fast approaching. The gods need to learn from their errors and have one final attempt at making man. It is the animals that guide them this time. The fox, the coyote, the parakeet and the raven all eat from the ripe yellow ears of maize in far-away fields in the lands known as Paxil and Cayala. They show gods the way to this fertile place, rich also with cacao, fruits and honey.

The divine Grandmother, Xmucane, grinds the maize and adds water to give it life. With the creation gods, they mould the plump, yellow flesh into human form and whisper invocations to bring it to life. Four men are made and shaped into being: the first is B'alam Quitze, the second is B'alam Aq'ab', the third is Majukutaj, and the fourth is Ik'i B'alam. These, then, are the ancestors of us all. The gods look on their creation and are finally happy with what they see. These four certainly look like men, they speak well and they clearly recognize the world around them.

'What can you see?' the gods ask the men. 'Do you know where you have come from?'

The men look about themselves, they see the earth that has been created and the vault of the sky above them. With true reverence, they address their gods: 'We are wholly grateful that you have created us. We can speak and see, we can wander the earth and consider the world around us. Thank you for everything you have made and the knowledge you have given us.' And finally, the creation gods were happy with what they had made.

THE DREAMTIME
ABORIGINAL AUSTRALIAN

In the beginning was the Dreamtime. It's an English word for the Aboriginal Australian concept of the creation time of the earth. It's a time of spirits and ancestral beings, inextricably linked to the land, eternal nature and rich cultural identity. The Dreaming (distinct from the Dreamtime) is a more general term that refers to the belief systems of the many First Nations of Australia.

While the Dreamtime tells of a beginning, the concept defies the passage of time. There is a sense of the Dreamtime being in the past, but simultaneously having always existed. It is at once the past, the present and the future.

In the creation story told here, the animals aren't created, but they merely emerge for the first time. The ancestral animals and spirits have always existed, and continue to exist in the animals and people alive today.

There are about five hundred different First Nations in Australia, each with their own legends, belief systems and languages. So, to lump any singular idea under the umbrella of Aboriginal Australian is inaccurate. However, one spirit that appears in the Dreaming of many First Nations is known as the Rainbow Serpent, and this gigantic snake has almost as many different names and stories as there are languages on the Australian continent. Sometimes male, sometimes female, this powerful being is often associated with the creation of the world, and the animals and people within it.

Some versions equate the Serpent with the long stretch of stars that make up our view of the Milky Way in the night sky, while others connect the snake with the iridescent rainbow during the daytime. The spirit is benevolent and life-giving, but can also bring danger and death. It is widely associated with winding valleys, and it commonly recognized as the bringer of rain, the maker of sinuous rivers and the guardian of watering holes.

You can learn more about how myths and legends travelled across the First Nations of Australia in Chapter 10: Songlines.

IN THE BEGINNING, THERE IS NOTHING

In a far, far-away time, the earth is dry, flat and empty. There are no animals that fill the land, no grass, no trees, no rivers or mountains, and certainly no people. One day, the mighty Rainbow Serpent awakes from an ancient slumber and looks about the barren earth. She goes in search of life, crossing the whole land from north to south and east to west in her unceasing quest. The Serpent's gigantic shape slithers sinuously across the land, gouging winding valleys through the earth, and forging mountains, hillsides and channels with each of her criss-crossing paths.

LIFE IS CREATED

Tired from her journeys, the Rainbow Serpent rests in a place far from where she started out. She decides that here is where life must be awoken. 'Now is your time, frogs,' the Serpent calls out. 'Come out from the ground!'

For the first time, the frogs emerge from the ground. They are heavy and slow, weighed down by their fill of water, which threatens to overflow. The Rainbow Serpent slithers about all of the frogs, tickling their vast, protruding bellies. In a moment, each of them pours forth a deluge of water that seems never to end. Torrents gush and flow across the land, filling the Serpent's meandering channels and valleys with brimming streams and watering holes.

As rivers drench the land, the earth starts to awaken

with grass, trees and colourful plants of all varieties. The Rainbow Serpent calls to the other animals: 'Kookaburra, wake up and bring us your laughter,' she commands. 'Lizards, wombats, kangaroos, emus and birds, now is the time.' One by one, all the animals rise up for the first time. Some fill the sea, others fly throughout the sky, and some animals live on the land. Each type of animal lives in perfect balance with the others, with enough water and the right amount of food for all of them.

THE LAW IS LAID DOWN

The Rainbow Serpent then brings in laws, and decrees that those who disobey them are to remain in their animal form, while those who are well-behaved may be upgraded to human form. Each community is given a totem of the animal from which they come as their identifying icon to remind them of their origins, and they may eat everything apart from their ancestral animal. In this way there will be enough on the land for everyone – a useful tenet to hold in a land where resources can be scarce.

As the bringer of water and life, the Rainbow Serpent is greatly respected by many of Australia's First Nations people. When approaching a watering hole, some may sing out to the Serpent on their way and rub a handful of earth into their bodies. Only by offering the right respect to the guardian of these waters may they drink.

Chapter 2
Death

aving tackled the question of the creation of the universe, a natural next uncertainty for our ancient ancestors to explain was that of death. Grief and loss are perhaps the most intense and confusing emotions that we can feel as humans. The disappearance of a beloved partner, parent or child from one moment to the next leaves those that remain with too many unanswered questions. The person has gone, but the body remains; it is logical that we create a distinction between the spiritual soul and the physical body that now is lifeless. If that is the case, then where does that soul go?

The finality of an eternal nothingness is too much for the grieving to comprehend, and so civilizations throughout the history of humanity have created elaborate and multifaceted mythologies about the afterlife. The stories bring comfort to the dying, provide answers for the living, and offer guidance on how to conduct our lives in the meantime.

Across the globe, many cultures split the world into distinct realms: the earthly realm for the living, the heavenly realm for the gods and the underworld for the dead. It makes sense to assign life-giving gods to the endless expanse of the skies, from where the sun, rain and seasons bring life and food to the world. Likewise, it feels logical to designate the world below us as the land of the dead, where many societies literally bury their deceased. The Norse religion, as noted earlier, had the world made up of the Yggdrasil tree, split into nine realms, the lower of which were associated with death and the afterlife. (See more on this in Chapter 1: Ragnarök.) The Greeks placed the judging god Hades in the dark depths of the Underworld, and the Romans did the same with their version of the same god, Pluto. From the Egyptians to the Mayans, it was the unseen netherworld that became the murky setting for our life after death.

The unique mythologies that arise to give explanation to this unavoidable aspect of life lead to the diverse variety of rituals and traditions surrounding death. The Egyptians mummified their dead and built great pyramids for their highest-ranking citizens to guide them into the afterlife. The Romans placed a coin in the mouth of their loved ones, so they would have spare change to give to Charon, the ferryman who would transport them over the River Styx in the Underworld. And in Ancient China, Emperor Qin Shi Huang was buried with a Terracotta Army of over eight thousand life-size soldiers, chariots and horses to guard him in the world beyond.

Throughout human history, death has been a subject that has captivated the imagination and has played a central role in the creation and evolution of many mythological systems. Whether it is seen as a journey to the afterlife, a way to achieve glory and honour, or a natural part of the cycle of life, death has always held a powerful and mysterious place in the human experience.

ORPHEUS AND EURYDICE
ROMAN

One of the greatest sorrows it is possible to endure must surely come from losing your husband or wife. This Roman tragedy tells of a desperately heartbroken man who was given the chance to step into the Underworld and to revive his wife back into the world of the living. Unhappily, not everything goes to plan. The tale of Orpheus and Eurydice is as much a story about love as it is about death, which is told in a number of versions in both Greek and Roman literature.

The Romans had a centuries-long love affair of their own with the culture, art, literature and architecture of the Greeks, and they copied as much of it as they could. Today, anything from Ancient Rome or Ancient Greece is categorized under the heading of *Classics*, because so much of their myths, religion and culture is shared. But it's worth noting that the two civilizations peaked at different points in history, and that it was the Romans who romanticized anything Greek as being weighty, ancient and part of their own origin story.

Ancient Greece *was* in fact ancient, even to Romans like Julius Caesar. When many of the monuments and buildings that you might now recognize in Rome were being constructed, they mimicked what to them was the Ancient Greek style. The Pantheon in Rome, for example, with its Corinthian columns rising to a triangular façade, was built so in about AD 126. That was nearly six hundred years after construction started on the Parthenon in Athens, from which it was arguably modelled. It's about as authentic as the Parthenon replica built in Nashville, Tennessee, in 1897.

This is how the Romans also dealt with the gods, myths and literature of Ancient Greece. They took the legends that had been passed down through word, inscription and pen, and retold them for a Roman audience. So, it is a Roman adaptation of this Greek tragedy that I retell, from the poet Ovid's *Metamorphoses*, written in AD 8.

A WEDDING AND A DEATH

Orpheus and Eurydice are hopelessly in love on their wedding day. Her beauty and wit are matched only by his talent for music. Orpheus has been gifted a lyre by Apollo, the god of music himself, and his dexterity spins melodies that have the very gods swooning. Hearing the man's captivating hymn play out from the couple's wedding party, Hymen, the god of marriage, appears to the crowd. Orpheus radiates as he plays. Surely, this must be a most auspicious blessing from the heavens for their union. Sadly, the opposite is true. No words of blessing come from Hymen's mouth. Everyone's face drops. The god's celebratory torch won't ignite, and instead billows out dark clouds of thick smoke that burns Orpheus' and Eurydice's eyes.

This is no good omen at all. And barely has the wedding finished, when Eurydice is bitten in the ankle by a snake. She dies instantly, and her soul descends to the Underworld.

JOURNEY INTO THE UNDERWORLD

Orpheus can mourn in the only way he knows: through the melodic lamentations of his lyre. The whole world and the heavens hear the aching grief in his music. But that's not enough! He must take his words down to the Underworld itself.

He travels through the gateway at Taenarus, known to be the entrance to the dark world below. Many had crossed its threshold, but it was almost unheard of that any had made their way back again. He passes crowds of the ghostly figures of bygone people, and the spirits of other buried lives. There, he encounters the king of the shadows, terrible Pluto, and his wife, Persephone.

He picks up his lyre and sings to them: 'Gods of the subterranean world, into which all of us mortals must fall, I can only bring you my absolute truth. I haven't come here to wander about the land of the dead, nor to slay the monstrous beasts that live here.' He continues his musical plea: 'I've come here because of my wife, snatched away so young by a venomous snake. I've tried to get on with my life, but I cannot. The god of love may not be so welcome down here, but I'm sure you two know his power.

'I beg you to show mercy. We all end up here in our final home, and you rule over us humans far longer than we ever spend alive in the upper world. But Eurydice's fate has been spun out too quickly – we haven't had the chance to live our lives together yet. When she's old and grey, when it's the right time, then she will come back to you. But ...' Orpheus' lyre pauses. 'If you can't allow this, then I won't return home either. You can have your pleasure in the death of two people.'

The heavenly music from Apollo's instrument, interwoven with Orpheus' melody and his heart-breaking story, brings the Underworld and all its eternal inhabitants to a standstill. Sisyphus, who has been condemned to push the same vast boulder up a mountainside indefinitely, for one moment lays aside his cursed rock. Tantalus, who has been sentenced to an eternity of fruit boughs that lift just out of reach and water that recedes when he bends down to drink, finally stops chasing the ebbing stream. Ixion, strapped to an endlessly spinning wheel with vultures pecking away at his liver as it perpetually grows back again and again, is brought to a stop by the sound of the song. The fading spirits weep openly, and even the terrible and vengeful Furies feel tears running down their hideous faces.

THE JOURNEY BACK TO THE
WORLD OF THE LIVING

Pluto and Persephone cannot help but be moved. They call for Eurydice, and name the conditions of her return: Orpheus must not set eyes on his wife until after they have crossed the threshold back into the world of the living. If he does, the gift will be lost forever. With his back turned to his most beloved wife, Orpheus begins the arduous and steep journey back home. They walk in a solemn silence, and the path is dark and misty. Occasionally, he can hear Eurydice struggle with the snake's wound still in her ankle. He wants nothing more than to turn and help her, and hurry her, and hold her. But Pluto's words echo in his ears.

As they finally near the margin of the upper world, Orpheus is suddenly overcome with a fear that she might not make it. She might slip at the final few steps; he might never see her again. In that moment, he turns his adoring and loving eyes. Instantly, Eurydice is snatched back into the depths. Orpheus stretches out his hands to catch her – or just to feel her. He reaches out and his hands touch nothing but cold air. In her final moment, dying for the second time, Eurydice feels the love in her husband's eyes and utters one word before she falls into the darkness: 'Goodbye.'

Orpheus can say nothing in return, as the unavoidable horror of his wife's double death penetrates every part of his body. She is gone. No matter how much longing breaks our hearts, it seems that death cannot be cheated.

ORPHEUS' VOW OF CHASTITY … SORT OF

For a whole week, Orpheus remains in the Underworld by the banks of the River Styx. He begs to be allowed to travel deeper to see the dark rulers again, but is refused. His only sustenance is his endless grief. Eventually returning to the world of the living, he spends three whole years shutting himself off from the love of another woman, despite being quite the catch with his god-given musical skill. The pureness of his chastity, we learn through Ovid's poem, is tarnished only by his love of young boys.

While horrific to the modern ear, this seems to be a practice referenced in much of Greek literature, which influenced Ovid's Latin poem. The young boys are often described in romantic, expressive and visual language that is quite different from how women are written about in Greek verse. The love for these boys – and their apparent love in return – is given as much romantic validity as some of the great adult love stories, if not more.

It seems mainly to occur in certain areas of Greece, and among the gods, heroes and well-to-do men of Greek and Roman literature. But perhaps it is that these characters represent more closely the audience who is writing and reading literature in those ancient times, and so other segments of society are written out of history.

ORPHEUS' DEATH

Orpheus' so-called chastity angers the local girls so much that when they spy him playing his lyre, one hurls a sharpened javelin directly towards his heart. Apollo's music, which plays through Orpheus' instrument, has attracted around him birds, beasts, and all manner of lush vegetation and fertile greenery. It proves to be a good shield from the missile. Another girl picks up a jagged rock, and with all her might, launches it at the man. This time, the heavenly magic of his music stops the rock in the air, and it falls to the ground.

The attack intensifies. More angry suitors gather ever closer to the singing bard. The birds around him are snatched from the air and their necks broken, the snakes and animals are all murdered. The missiles rain down on him, and the first rock is reddened by his blood. The wild girls pick up the rakes and harrows of nearby farmers, who have fled from the frenzied mob, and swoop on Orpheus like a pack of frothing dogs on a helpless stag. He is brutally killed and his body is left to float down the river.

When he reaches the Underworld, Orpheus searches everywhere for his wife, and they are finally reunited. He surrounds her with his devoted arms, and never needs to let go of her again throughout eternity. They lovingly walk side by side, and sometimes he steps ahead of her to look back – reassuringly – at his cherished wife.

IZANAMI IN YOMI
JAPANESE

The legend of Izanami is not for the fainthearted. Gory from the start and heart-breaking to the end, it tells of the creation of Japan and the world by the goddess Izanami and her husband (and brother) Izanagi. The goddess is simultaneously associated with creation and with death and destruction, and this story of her descent into the Underworld, known as Yomi, explains how that came to be.

This version of the legend of Izanami is told in the

Japanese collection of myths known as *Kojiki*, or *The Records of Ancient Matters*. The anthology was committed to writing in AD 711 by Ō no Yasumaro, a nobleman to the empress, but the legends it describes were passed down by generations through word and writing for decades – if not hundreds of years – beforehand.

In this myth, you may notice some remarkable similarities with the tale of Orpheus and Eurydice (see page 34): both couples are deeply in love, both are separated by death soon after they marry, and both husbands must resist the urge to look upon their dead bride in the Underworld. As with many myths about death and the underworld from a wide range of mythologies, this legend is a poignant reminder that we cannot cheat death despite our deepest yearning. Very few mythologies depict humans travelling into the underworld and making it back in one piece, and this Japanese tale doesn't even offer that luxury to a god and goddess who are deeply in love.

IZANAMI'S DEATH

Izanami, the goddess of creation, is in agony. Through the union with her husband Izanagi, she has given birth to the eight divine islands that make up the Japanese archipelago. Now, more islands are created and gods are born from their holy coupling: one god dedicated to the frothing sea, another to the rushing winds, another to the life-giving trees, one dedicated to the earth, another to the heavens. Dozens of deities spring forth from Izanami, and from each of them further generations are born.

One birth injures the maternal goddess: it is the fire god Kagutsuchi blazing forth, searing Izanami from the inside out. She screams out in agony and vomits from the pain. Two more gods materialize from her vomit, two more climb from her faeces, and a further two emerge from her urine. Finally, she can do no more. Having given birth to fourteen islands and thirty-five deities, the goddess of creation is overcome by a sacred death.

Izanagi is beside himself with grief. 'Oh, my beautiful Izanami!' he cries. 'Why have I had to give up my wonderful wife in exchange for this one child that has scalded you?' In abject agony, he collapses to the floor, crawling towards her feet, then her head, whereupon he falls wretchedly upon her and sobs, and from his outpouring tears is born a goddess of lamentation.

THE LAND OF THE DEAD

Izanagi buries his beloved wife, and his anger towards the fire god Kagutsuchi only grows with his grief. He seeks out the murderous offspring, and lifts up his mighty, shimmering sword in anticipation of vengeance. With one swipe, he cuts off Kagutsuchi's head. Thick, red blood splatters a clean line across the rocks, from which emerge gods dedicated to the earth. Izanagi, breathing heavily after the swift killing, holds the sword high. From the weapon's razor-sharp blade, heavy gore drips down to the ground and gods of fire and speed are born. Blood soaks down the sword and drenches his fingers, from which are born two more deities.

Broken by his grief, Izanagi must see his beloved wife once more. As her soul passes down into the Underworld, Yomi, he follows down that long, treacherous path, and calls out her name again and again into the gloomy land of the dead. From the great hall of Yomi, a shape appears at the door. Could this be his treasured Izanami?

'My darling!' Izanagi calls out. 'Come back to me! We have so much more of the world to create.'

'It's you!' Izanami responds. 'You're too late, my love. I have already eaten from the fruits of Yomi. It's so amazing that you've made it here. Let me go and speak with the gods of Yomi – I have to let them know how much I desire to return with you. But there's one important thing, darling,' she continues. 'You mustn't set eyes on me down here, I beg you.' With that, her dark shape fades back inside the palace of the dead.

Izanagi waits for her return, but a long time passes and he is still alone in this dreadful place. He waits a little longer, but grows worried and impatient. He wants nothing more than to be with his beloved wife. Pacing up and down, looking again and again at the door she last appeared in, Izanagi cannot contain his anguish. He takes the comb from his hair and breaks off one of its wooden teeth. As he approaches the bleak and gloomy portal, he lights the wooden splinter and steps inside. Izanagi has broken the strict taboo.

In the flashing firelight, his wife's corpse stands before him, maggots writhing and squirming over her rotting flesh. In her head, breasts and belly, the gods of fire and black thunder are released. In her loins, the god of shattering thunder is created, and from each hand and foot another colossal god of reverberating thunder booms out a dreadful sound.

Izanagi stumbles back in utter horror at the sight and turns to flee far away from this terrible place, and his wife screams out after him: 'You have broken the promise! You have shamed me!' At once, Izanami is changed, and she releases hideous spirits to pursue him. Izanagi runs for his life away from these deadly witches. He pulls the band of vine from his hair and throws it behind him; immediately grapes spring up from the ground. The spirits stop to eat, giving him a few moments to get ahead of his pursuers.

As they catch up with him again, Izanagi takes the comb from his hair and casts it into the earth; immediately towering bamboo shoots rise from the ground. The spirits stop to eat once more. Flashing his mighty sword as he retreats, the horrified god makes it at last to the gateway out of Yomi. He takes one last look back to see the terrible demon that was his wife surging towards him. Izanagi lifts a gargantuan bolder and blocks the pass to the Underworld.

Now facing one another, on either side of the great rock, the two gods who were once so much in love break their bond. 'I promise you,' Izanami calls out from the Underworld, 'that I will strangle to death a thousand of your population every single day for the rest of eternity.'

'And I promise you,' Izanagi responds from the upper world, 'that every single day, I will see to it that one and a half thousand of my people are born.'

This is why the population keeps growing, because for all those who are called down to Yomi in their death, even more are brought to the land of the living.

OSIRIS
EGYPTIAN

In about 2350 BC, someone etched hieroglyphic symbols of birds, beetles, eyes, shapes and emblems into the inside walls of a pyramid in Saqqara, Egypt, about 15 kilometres south of the more famous Sphinx and pyramids at Giza. Countless lines of the mysterious symbols were uncovered across Egypt, and it wasn't until more than four thousand years later that they were deciphered in the early AD 1800s. The art of creating meaning from a series of unfamiliar symbols is nothing short of a code-breaking miracle, and it means that more than four millennia later, you can read that same story in this chapter that the ancient stone-etcher was telling.

In fact, the Egyptians had been around for nearly a further one thousand years before the story you'll read here was inscribed. Their rich civilization has inspired schoolchildren and archaeologists alike, with the preservation of mummies, pyramids, pharaohs and the Sphinx over so many thousands of years making this a truly unparalleled ancient culture.

The modern-era fascination with Egyptian mythology blossomed with the excavation and opening of Tutankhamun's tomb by archaeologist Howard Carter in 1922. As a result of a few calamities and deaths in his team following that excavation, the present-day myth of the Curse of the Pharaohs was born. A British financer of the excavation died from a mosquito bite in Cairo. The media went into a frenzy, and reports travelled around the world of a curse. Another Egyptologist claimed his house had burnt down because of his visit to the tomb, while others flung Egyptian artefacts from their homebound ships to stave off the curse.

At the very least, this readiness to concoct ancient curses may have come from a natural guilt response to the trend of British archaeologists looting the world's relics and tombs. If nothing else, it demonstrates the power of legend in how we make sense of the inexplicable. Humanity finds it easier to create ancient spirits and vengeful gods than to accept sudden death and indiscriminate suffering. It is this twentieth-century invention of the Curse of the Pharaohs that retains a strong connotation for modern interpretations of the Ancient Egyptians, from video games to the mummies of movies and cartoons.

Much of what we understand of Egyptian mythology has had to be pieced together from disparate hieroglyphic sources, most of which are incomplete, and many of which tell different variations of the same story. It is a testament to the oral tradition of storytelling, where each narrator, each generation and each region adds their own details and embellishments to ancient tales as they pass them on. The story of Osiris includes his own murder, but not much is written about how it came about. The Egyptians imbued great significance into the physical act of writing, and believed their hieroglyphics were more than just text; the engravings were thought to bring the myths into existence. Other belief systems, such as Hinduism and Judaism, put a similar weight on the significance of the physical words and shapes in their scriptures, believing written language to be a god-given form of communication. With hieroglyphics holding such power for the Egyptians, the exact details of the murder of the god Osiris remain largely untold.

ORDER IS BROUGHT TO THE WORLD

In the beginning, there is nothing. Just the watery chaos and disorder of the god Nun fills the universe. The ruler of all the gods, Ra, emerges. The sky goddess Nut and the earth god Geb are separated, and the world is created. Chaotic Nun is cast aside to beyond the borders of the universe, and in his place is left a wonderful sense of balance, justice and cosmic harmony, known as *Ma'at*. This principle of universal truth is present in all elements of Egyptian life, informing their morality, their understanding of cosmology, as well as their laws and politics.

OSIRIS IS KILLED

There comes a time when the son of Geb and Nut becomes the ruler of all Egypt. His name is Osiris, and he rules the people well, alongside his queen Isis. But an indiscretion triggers a wild jealousy in his brother, Set. Osiris sleeps with their sister Nephthys – lover of Set. The resentful brother flies into a fit of rage and cuts Osiris into dozens of pieces. At that very moment, Queen Isis hears a terrible lament echo across the whole land.

OSIRIS IS RESURRECTED

Hearing that Set has scattered his brother's chopped-up remains over all of Egypt, Isis and Nephthys take on the form of kite birds and set out on a mission to seek these out. As they fly, the whole of Egypt hears the wailing cry of the kite birds, calling out in grief. Isis' tears fall down on the land, causing the mighty Nile to swell in its course. To this day, the river floods its plains with a rich and fertile deluge each year to commemorate Isis' grief and Osiris' resurrection.

The goddesses retrieve the pieces of their beloved husband and brother, and with the help of the dog-god Anubis, they restore him to his former state. Osiris becomes the first being of Egypt to be mummified, a practice carried out to stop the decay of death in its tracks and to retain the dead in the state that their loved ones want to remember them in. Taking up his new position in the realm of the dead, Osiris sires an heir to his throne. His rule of Egypt remains eternal in the continuation of his family line, as well as the fertility that his scattered body provided to all the regions of the land.

Chapter 3
Gods and Goddesses

any world mythologies have a rich and seemingly endless character list of gods, goddesses and spirits, whose actions in the heavens directly impact on the fate of mortals on earth. In Greek mythology, the deadly ten-year War of Troy was instigated in part because of the three goddesses Hera, Athena and Aphrodite fighting over who was the most beautiful. In Mesopotamian mythology, it was the scheming gods Enlil, Ninurta and Annugi who decided to send a huge flood upon the earth to rid it of its people, and it was the benevolent god Ea who saved humanity by advising Utnapishtim to build a great ark. (See more about that story in Chapter 10: Gilgamesh and the Great Flood.)

It is remarkable to note that many of the same characters pop up in polytheistic cultures around the world. In various civilizations that have not had any contact, you find the father of all other gods. Whether it's the Egyptian Ra, the Greek Zeus or the Norse Odin, he is often associated with the sky, creation and judgement. He is often accompanied by a mother goddess, more associated with the earth and nature. Almost all such religions have a god who looks after the dead: the Norse goddess Hel, the Greek Hades and the Japanese Izanami (see Chapter 2: Izanami in Yomi). A god of love, one of war, one of harvest and nature, one of the sea, and ones to guide the sun and the moon are frequent characters.

The purpose of these countless deities in myth is to help humanity make sense of a confusing world. Unable to rationalize the brutality of death, the high ecstasy of love, the cruelty of famine or the destruction of floods, we created legends of all-powerful, mighty gods to both entertain us in our suffering, and provide explanations for the incomprehensible.

It's far easier – and far more interesting – to hear a story about warring gods, love-stricken deities and jealous overlords than it is to accept some of the adversity that humanity experiences without explanation. Unpredictable gods representing love, fear, rumour, deceit, wealth, war and weather were responsible for all those things we simply couldn't explain. Many civilizations thus created anthropomorphic representations of some of the highs and lows that they experienced in life. In Ancient Greece, for example, the name of the love god Eros simply means *Love* in Greek, and so it is sometimes deliberately vague in ancient texts as to whether someone is acting under the influence of the emotion of love or under the influence of the god *Love*.

The myths in this chapter speak of two different societies, and how the gods in their pantheons helped explain the world to the people who told those stories, and led to rituals and religious practices to gain a sense of control over the unpredictability of ancient life.

ESHU

YORUBA

Eshu is the trickster god of the Yoruba people, who originate in Nigeria, Benin and Togo. Their rich culture and mythology travelled with the enslaved people of Africa, and so Eshu's stories are found under various names and versions in Cuba, Brazil and beyond. As one of the primary *orishas*, the spirits and deities of the Yoruba religion, Eshu acts as the messenger of the gods. As such, he is the gatekeeper between the physical and spiritual worlds, and anyone seeking a path to the Yoruba pantheon must first come through Eshu. He becomes the go-to god for prayers and rituals, in the hope that he will pass on the messages to the other *orishas* and to the supreme spirit of the heavens, Olodumare.

Eshu is responsible for protecting rituals, offering protection to worshippers, and providing moral guidance. But there is something more intriguing about him, as he is one of the more complex figures in mythology. He is the embodiment of mischief, causing chaos, disorder and harm to innocent people. At the same time, he himself is the epitome of orderliness. The god in charge of law enforcement and order spreads chaos among humanity, perhaps so that we may understand and appreciate the order that he governs. Both structure and discord in one mischievous god.

While he, on the one hand, sparks arguments between lovers and friends, Eshu's purpose is to bring balance to humanity. His tricks and pranks often are used to teach his victims a lesson concerning morality. On earth, the unpredictable god is to be found at every crossroads, ready to bring confusion, uncertainty and hardship, while simultaneously acting as the protector of travellers. Today, red pillars of laterite rock or mud are found at the entrances to some Yoruba villages, markets and homes as a totem to Eshu and a focus for prayers of protection. In this story, we hear how Eshu becomes the messenger and gatekeeper to the heavens.

OLODUMARE'S GARDEN

The Supreme Being, Olodumare, is the queen of the heavens. Her beautiful gardens are known among all the *orishas* for their rich, fertile soil and bountiful fruit and vegetables, which grow bigger and tastier than anywhere else in existence. One sunny afternoon, the young trickster Eshu manages to find his way into the sacred gardens. He bounds around the oasis, delighting in the delicious fact that he has gone unnoticed. He explores the verdant bushes bursting with berries, and marvels at the vast fronds towering over him. Eventually, he comes to the purpose of his trespass: at the far end of the garden he spies the unmistakably luscious leaves of Olodumare's yams.

Ecstatic at his find, Eshu fills his pockets with the delicious and plump roots of the yam. He cannot wait to devour them. But then, a troubling thought crosses his mind: what if he is caught? He'll be banished from the heavens! He must find a clever ruse to cover his footsteps, and he thinks he knows just the way.

ESHU'S TRICK

Eshu looks about him, suddenly keener than before not to be detected. He scurries along the edge of the garden with his eyes darting about. Eventually, he comes to where the Supreme Being Olodumare is snoozing among the winding roots of a vast, shady tree. Eshu creeps up and snatches the two large slippers that lie next to the sleeping god, before quickly returning to the yam patch. It is scattered with earth and dotted with obvious holes where the yams once grew. This evidence might give Eshu away, except that the trickster now uses Olodumare's slippers to make clear footprints in the vegetable bed. One step after the other, unmistakably leading to the absent yams and away again.

OLODUMARE'S WRATH

Upon waking, Olodumare steps into her slippers – not noticing the clumps of mud on their soles – and takes her customary stroll about the sumptuous gardens. Even from a distance, it is clear that something is amiss with the yams. Brown earth is littered about the otherwise pristine pathway, and there are several hollow spaces where the prized roots most definitely used to be. Who would dare cause such mischief at the very heart of the heavens? Olodumare summons all of the *orishas* to her gardens. They know that this sort of request is less of an invitation and more of a subpoena for a divine wrongdoing.

'Who has dared to steal from my garden?' the Supreme Being thunders across all the *orishas*. 'Which one of you broke in and disrespected me like this?' Eshu is peering about with guilty joy. Look at all this chaos! Look how Olodumare lays down the laws that have been broken! Look at the fear on all their faces!

Just as Eshu is contemplating all this disorder he has created, his eyes meet Olodumare's. Her truculent gaze is bearing down on him. Eshu looks down, and realizes that his hoard of stolen yams is clearly visible through the pockets of his trousers. There is no wriggling out of this one.

ESHU'S PUNISHMENT

Olodumare speaks directly to the god: 'If you're so keen to visit me up in the heavens, Eshu, I have the perfect punishment.'

Olodumare's sentence is that Eshu must visit her up in the skies at the end of each day to pass on the news of everything that has happened then on earth. In this way, Eshu is made the messenger of the gods, the guardian of the path for all prayers to heaven, and the protector of all gateways and crossroads.

RAMA AND SITA
INDIAN

The story of Rama and Sita is told in one of the oldest and longest epic poems of the world, the *Ramayana*. The title refers to the journey – physical and spiritual – of its hero prince Rama, whose wife Sita is kidnapped by the demon king Ravana. Alongside the *Mahabharata* (see Chapter 8: The *Bhagavad Gita*), it is one of the most important and widely read epics in Hindu mythology. It is a legend that was passed down through the generations before being committed to writing. As such, it is believed to have been composed over time, perhaps as early as the eighth century BC (around the same time as Homer's epic poems *The Iliad* and *The Odyssey* in Greece), and to have been continually developed up to the third century AD.

The *Ramayana* is not just a myth, but a vast literary work that exists in a number of forms, with versions remaining an important part of the mythologies of India, Cambodia, Indonesia, Malaysia and beyond. Its 24,000 verses are divided into seven *khandas* or books, each telling a different part of Rama's story. In addition to the narrative, it also includes philosophical teachings on the duty, destiny and spiritual journey of humanity.

It is attributed to the author Valmiki, who is said to have been inspired to write the epic after witnessing a hunter kill a male crane bird that was in the act of courting its female mate. The female cried out in terror and died from the shock. Valmiki's compassion for the bird and his condemnation of the hunter's actions are said to have moved him to compose the *Ramayana* as a cautionary tale against the consequences of harming innocent beings.

The *Ramayana* has had a profound impact on Indian culture and society. It has served as a source of moral guidance, inspiring generations to uphold values such as loyalty, duty and compassion. The character of Rama, in particular, has been held up as a paragon of virtue, and his story has been used to teach children about the importance of following the path of righteousness. The *Ramayana* has also inspired countless works of art, from paintings and sculptures to music and dance performances.

Despite its ancient origins, the *Ramayana* remains a vital part of Indian culture today. Its themes and lessons continue to resonate with people of all ages and backgrounds, and the story has been adapted and reinterpreted in countless ways. Its enduring popularity is a testament to its timeless message of the triumph of good over evil, and its ability to speak to the human experience across cultures and centuries.

In this story of Rama and Sita, we encounter a monkey king, Hanuman, not to be confused with the Monkey King, Sun Wukong, of Chinese mythology. (See Chapter 5: The Monkey King.)

FOUR HEIRS ARE BORN

In the ancient city of Ayodha, King Dashratha is troubled. Despite having three wives, he has no son and heir to whom he can pass on the crown. Desperate, he implores the gods to grant him a son. The gods hear his sacrifice and prayers, and it is the Supreme Being Vishnu himself who chooses to come to earth in human form. He has heard that the demon god Ravana is terrorizing the world and disrupting sacred traditions, and so he resolves to tackle Ravana himself. As such, Vishnu is incarnated as the prince Rama, a son to the king's wife, Kaushalya. Sons are also granted to King Dashratha's two other wives. Sumitra gives birth to twins: Shatrughna, and Rama's lifelong companion, Lakshman; and Kaikeyi gives birth to the youngest prince, Bharat.

When Rama grows into a young man, he and Lakshman are called as skilled fighters to help destroy evil demons in far-off kingdoms. On their journey, they come to the city of Mithila, ruled by King Janaka. The king tells them of his legendary bow, which is so strong that no one has been able to string it successfully. Only the man who is able to do so will get his daughter's hand in marriage. Rama proves his divine strength and is able not only to string the bow, but to split it in two. The princess Sita is married to the hero.

JEALOUSY AND A PROMISE

Dashratha is delighted with the turn of events. Finally he can pass down the throne to the oldest son and his new bride. However, one of the king's wives is jealous of the newly-wed couple. Queen Kaikeyi, the mother of the youngest prince Bharat, wants the crown for her own son, and manipulates Dashratha to honour a promise he made her many years beforehand to grant two wishes.

The first wish, Kaikeyi tells him, is for her son Bharat to become the king of Ayodha. The second wish is that Rama be banished to the forest for fourteen years. Kaikeyi reasons that this should be long enough for Bharat to establish his role on the throne. Conflicted by love for his son Rama and the need to deliver on the promises he made, Dashratha gives in. Rama takes his banishment with calm acceptance, and is followed by his cherished wife Sita and loyal brother Lakshman. Crushed by the grief of losing his treasured son, King Dashratha dies.

THE DEMON KING SETS HIS EYES ON SITA

Rama and Sita enjoy a happy and simple life living off the land and the forest for many years, together with Lakshman. After over a decade of their making the best of their exile, the demon god Ravana sets his eyes on Sita and decides he will take her away from Rama. Ravana is a terrifying figure with twenty strong arms and ten frightful heads. If he is to deceive the princess, he must go in disguise, and so he assumes the form of a beautiful golden deer and wanders towards the couple's woodland home.

Sita is so entranced by the dazzling creature that she asks her husband to capture it for her. Rama senses that demons are at play here, but he cannot change Sita's mind, so he asks Lakshman to guard his beloved wife as he chases the shining animal deep into the forest. Not long afterwards, they hear a cry from far off: Rama is hurt! Sita pleads with Lakshman to go to her husband's aid; Rama needs his protection more than she does.

The loyal Lakshman acquiesces, and commands Sita to stay safely inside their home. He draws a divine circle of protection around the home, inside of which she cannot be harmed, and he nervously goes in search of his brother.

SITA IS KIDNAPPED

Now that Sita is alone, the demon god Ravana steals his opportunity. Taking the form of a wise holy man, he is able to entice Sita out of her home and beyond the line of protection. In that moment as she steps over the line, he reveals his gruesome identity and grabs the screaming Sita into his chariot, which is drawn high into the sky by flying demons. Terrified for her life, Sita focuses her mind to think rationally. As they soar higher above the forest and further away, the princess drops pieces of her jewellery to leave a trail in the hope that her husband may find her.

When met by his brother, Rama soon realizes that they have all been tricked. He rushes desperately back to their home, but his worst fears have been realized: Sita has been taken.

HANUMAN'S ARMY ATTACKS

Rama spots the trail of jewellery and begins his long quest to find his wife. He soon meets Hanuman, the gleaming white Monkey King himself, who resolves to help Rama in his search for Sita. Search parties are sent to the far reaches of the world in all directions, though these have little luck in finding the princess, but Hanuman's search reveals she is being held on the island of Lanka. He flies over to the island to attest to her location, and brings back her comb as proof to Rama that she is there and ready to be rescued.

Rama and Hanuman gather together a vast monkey army to conquer Ravana's kingdom. They build a gigantic floating bridge from grass, sand and sacred rocks, and the animals pour over onto the island. There, they are met in equal match by Ravana's fearsome warriors and a long, bloody battle takes place. Many are lost on both sides, until eventually Rama and Ravana meet in combat.

Skilled though he is, Rama struggles to overcome Ravana's twenty thrashing arms. Each time he's able to cut off one of the demon's terrible heads, a new one grows back in its place. Eventually, he pulls from his quiver a divine arrow and takes aim at the hideous Ravana. Rama chants a prayer as the arrow flies and hits the demon king and kills him directly.

LIGHTS GUIDE THE WAY

As the war comes to an end, the lovers are finally reunited. Conflicted by his love for Sita and by tradition,

Rama initially is convinced to reject his wife. Ravana has repeatedly tried to seduce her, and Rama questions Sita's honour and purity. Bereft, the princess asks loyal Lakshman to build a burning pyre and seeks guidance from the god Agna. In a grand display of bravery and devotion, Sita enters the towering inferno to prove her devotion. And yet, she does not burn. Agna carries the princess out of the flames unharmed and bears witness to her fidelity.

The world rejoices at the defeat of Ravana, and the triumph of good over evil. Rama and Sita's exile is finally over and they can make the long journey home to Ayodha. The citizens of the kingdom light lamps in every home and along every path to help the couple find their way safely back. Even today, Hindus across the world light lamps or *diyas* at Diwali to celebrate good triumphing over evil and light winning over darkness.

Chapter 4
Heroes and Heroines

o legend is complete without a hero or heroine at the helm of the narrative. Often bold, brave and strong, they are the main characters in the poems, novels and folklore that shape mythologies. Sometimes reluctant to take on the title of hero in their own story, they find themselves on a grand mission to save their people, their family or themselves. Their journeys are both physical and spiritual, from which they emerge tougher and wiser. (You can read more about the physical journey many heroes embark on in Chapter 10: Epic Journeys.)

Sometimes heroes are superhuman in strength, like the chiselled Greek demigod Hercules, and sometimes they appear as the everyday person who chooses to do extraordinary things, like the Ancient Chinese rural-daughter-turned-warrior Mulan. What unites all mythological heroes, however, is what they can teach us about ourselves. They act as an allegorical character to represent a particular aspect of the human psyche and to inspire listeners to achieve great things. Through hearing how they overcome fears, outwit enemies, behead monsters, and – almost always – come out victorious, the audience to their legends are made to wonder what is possible in their own lives.

The heroes of ancient tales are, pleasingly, not always perfect. They have flaws, fears and selfish urges. Hercules murders his whole family (see below), Roman hero Aeneas forgets his god-sent mission because he'd rather roll around with the beautiful Queen Dido (see Chapter 6), and Greek hero Odysseus adds many years onto his journey home because of his own cockiness (see Chapter 10). Unlike many of the heroes of present-day movies, ancient protagonists can be narcissistic and unreasonable. Through their imperfections, however, we can learn so much more about what it takes to achieve heroic feats.

HERCULES
GREEK AND ROMAN

Hercules is the archetypal mythological hero: bulging muscles, as brave as an ox, and no stranger to death-defying adventure.

He is the son of Zeus, king of the gods, who sired dozens of offspring outside of his marriage to queen of the gods, Hera. Zeus was so taken by the mortal woman Alcmene that he disguised himself as her husband, and the result of their union was Hercules and twin brother Iphicles.

Hera's jealousy and anger at her husband's infidelity is often taken out on his illegitimate children – about 115 of them – and Hercules seems to bear the brunt of her wrath. When he still a baby, the vengeful goddess places two large snakes into the twins' cot, to be rid of them both. But while Iphicles cowers in a corner and screams out, Hercules calmly picks up both snakes and strangles them. His mother comes to the cot to find him playing with them like two limp dolls. He is clearly no ordinary young boy.

Hera's anger could not be mollified, even if the child was named in her honour – his Greek name, Heracles, literally means *the glory of Hera*. In this book, I will use his Roman name, Hercules, as it is more familiar to our ears. When he grows into adulthood, Hera drives Hercules into a mad frenzy, in which he kills his wife and children. Horrified and sickened by his own actions, he seeks forgiveness and advice from the wise Oracle of Delphi. It is decreed that Hercules must enter a decade of servitude under King Eurystheus of Tiryns, and must undertake any task that the king orders.

This is hardly an even playing field, as King Eurystheus is an accomplice of Hera – she had orchestrated him being coronated rather than Hercules. The embittered goddess is in the king's ear to set a series of impossible tasks for the demigod to perform, with the aim of ensuring his complete failure.

THE TWELVE LABOURS OF HERCULES

Pieced together from a range of Greek and Roman literature, the Labours of Hercules are the seemingly insurmountable challenges that King Eurystheus sets for the hero. Originally a list of ten trials for Hercules to undertake, it was extended to twelve after two of his achievements were deemed as cheating by the incredulous king. The completion of the tasks would cleanse his soul and propel him into immortality.

Undertaking a *Herculean task* is still used today to describe a difficult or impossible challenge. The Labours of Hercules mainly involve him killing or taming wildly ferocious mythical creatures. Some of these beasts were commemorated as constellations in the Roman zodiac, and others are believed to be related to those creatures described in the ancient night sky. It is possible, therefore, that the purpose of these myths about Hercules was to make sense of the stars. Hercules himself was given a dedication in the skies, a constellation that retains his name to this day.

1. KILLING THE NEMEAN LION

Hercules' first impossible task is to kill a gigantic and ferocious lion that has been causing havoc around Nemea. Its claws are made of solid bronze, and its skin cannot be pierced. Hercules finds that his arrows, despite their precision, are unable to penetrate the lion's hide. He takes up his mighty club and beats the beast, driving it back into a confined cave. Here, the hero is able to grab hold of the writhing head of the cornered animal and strangle it until it struggles no more. The image of Hercules with his club in one hand and the lion skin draped majestically over his shoulder is one that is repeated over and over in classical art.

King Eurystheus is so terrified by the sight of Hercules returning from his first Labour, with the undefeatable lion defeated, that he hides away and bars him from ever entering the city again.

2. KILLING THE LERNAEAN HYDRA

Hercules' second impossible mission is to kill the hideous Hydra, which guards an entrance to the Underworld in the lake of Lerna. In classical mythology, anything to do with the Underworld is certainly not to be trifled with; this is serious business. The Hydra is a monstrous, nine-headed sea snake, offspring of the mother of all monsters, Echidna, and sibling of the three-headed dog Cerberus. This Echidna is half-woman, half-snake, rather than the cute – but spiky – Australian mammal that bears her name. Each time Hercules cuts one of the Hydra's heads off, two more grow in its place, making the task increasingly challenging and perilous.

With the help of his nephew Iolaus, Hercules devises a plan to set a burning torch onto the severed necks of the Hydra, cauterizing the wounds and preventing further heads from growing. Hera's vengeful eyes look on, and she sends a giant crab in an attempt to help turn the losing battle, but Hercules swiftly does away with this by crushing it underfoot. Finally defeating the Hydra, he dips his arrows into its poisonous blood, and uses these to great effect in some of the later Labours and beyond. In Hera's grief at the loss of both creatures, she sets the Hydra and Cancer constellations into the stars.

3. CAPTURING THE CERYNEIAN HIND

The next challenge is to capture the enormous, golden-horned deer of Ceryneia, an animal sacred to the goddess Artemis. King Eurystheus is convinced that, even if Hercules is able to get the animal, Artemis would not spare him for stealing her property. One statue of Artemis, found in Ephesus in modern-day Turkey, has her adorned with what looks like dozens of bull's testicles. She is clearly not one to mess about with.

Hercules chases the hind for an entire year before he finally gets his hands on it. Artemis is predictably enraged by his presumption, not least because he breaks off one of the deer's golden horns in the struggle. However, Hercules is able to win the goddess round, and she allows him to borrow the animal for the sake of succeeding in his Labours, after which he must set it free.

4. CAPTURING THE ERYMANTHIAN BOAR

This huge and deadly beast is next on King Eurystheus' list – surely this unpredictable and violent boar that has killed so many cannot be defeated. However, Hercules chases the animal around the sides of Mount Erymanthos until he drives it into deep snow, where he captures it in a net to bring back to Eurystheus. The king is so terrified at the sight of Hercules with the massive creature slung over his shoulders that he leaps into a large bronze jar to hide.

5. CLEANING THE AUGEAN STABLES

The next Labour – presumably set from within the bronze jar – sees a shift from deadly beasts to humiliation. King Augeas of Elis has a huge herd of three thousand cattle, and Hercules' task is to muck out the stables – a duty that has been overlooked for three whole decades.

Augeas makes a deal with Hercules to gift him one-tenth of his mighty herd if the hero can complete the revolting task in one day. Blessed with brains as well as brawn, Hercules diverts two nearby rivers, the Apheus and the Peneus, to flow directly through the stables and wash away the dung in one great deluge. Augeas doesn't keep his side of the bargain, however, which enrages Hercules. After he completes his Labours, he attacks the city of Elis and kills Augeas, before handing the city back to the king's exiled son. It is said that Hercules started the first Olympic Games in celebration of the victory over Elis.

6. KILLING THE STYMPHALIAN BIRDS

Around Lake Stymphalis in Arcadia are flocks of man-eating birds. Each has a solid bronze beak and feathers that can be fired like arrows, and killing these birds is Hercules' sixth Labour. The goddess Athena comes to Hercules' aid, by commissioning a bronze rattle to be forged by the gods' own blacksmith, Hephaestus. Through this noisy contraption, the birds are startled up into the air, where they are an easy target for Hercules.

It is thought they are memorialized in the bird constellations Aquila and Cygnus, the eagle and swan, which lie in the night sky either side of Sagitta, representing Hercules' arrows.

7. CAPTURING THE CRETAN BULL

This huge white bull was sent to Crete by god of the sea Poseidon, and seduced King Minos' wife Pasiphaë. She even had a fake wooden cow constructed that she could hide inside to fulfil her questionable desires, as the result of which, she mothered the half-man, half-beast Minotaur. Hercules' mission is to capture the gigantic beast and to bring it back to Tiryns to be offered to Hera as a sacrifice. She rebuffs the offer and the bull is released again, after which it is commemorated in the Taurus constellation.

8. TAKING THE MARES OF DIOMEDES

Next in Hercules' tasks is to steal the four man-eating horses of King Diomedes. Eurystheus was convinced that either the horses or the violent king would finally rid him of this seemingly indestructible man. The horses are tethered by thick iron chains, and froth at the mouth as Hercules and several of his young companions approach. Unaware of quite how bloodthirsty they are, Hercules leaves one of his young companions, Abderus, to look after the horses while he and the others dispatch King Diomedes. They return to find Abderus killed. Hercules holds the body in his arms and weeps, before creating a tomb for the boy – upon which site years later the city of Abdera is founded.

Another version of this myth sees Hercules feeding Diomedes to his own horses, removing the threat of the savage king and, at the same time, calming the horses enough to be able to muzzle them and bring them back to the increasingly incredulous King Eurystheus.

9. OBTAINING THE GIRDLE OF HIPPOLYTA

Hippolyta is queen of the Amazons, a notorious clan of fierce female warriors. In Ancient Greece, their name was rumoured to mean *breastless*, a reference to these expert archers cutting off one breast so as to shoot their bows with more accuracy. There is no evidence of this in ancient art or literature, but it vividly illustrates how they were viewed as single-minded and ruthless fighters.

Hippolyta is the owner of a belt made by Ares, the god of war. Eurystheus wants to present the girdle to his own daughter, or will accept Hercules' death as a happy second prize. At the outset, this Labour looks quite easy. Hippolyta is obliging and quite willing to hand over the belt to Hercules. Hera steps in once again, and spreads the rumour among the Amazons that Hercules is not only after the girdle, but after the queen herself. The Amazons need little provocation to attack Hercules, during which fight he ends up killing Hippolyta and stealing her belt.

10. OBTAINING THE CATTLE OF GERYON

Geryon is a three-headed, three-bodied monster, and owner of a herd of cows coloured red by the setting sun of the west. Stealing this cattle is the aim of Hercules' next task. The hero sails to the island of Erytheia, where he beats to death the two-headed guard dog Orthrus with his trusty club, and uses an arrow dipped in the blood of the Hydra to kill monstrous Geryon. The journey back with the majestic herd is not achieved lightly either, with Hera placing a horsefly in the herd to disrupt and disperse them – but our hero of course succeeds in the end.

At the completion of the original ten Labours, Eurystheus feels there is no option but to change the rules. He discounts two of Hercules' achievements: the killing of the Hydra was done with the help of Iolaus, and by agreeing payment for cleaning the Augean Stables in the form of one-tenth of King Augeas' herd, he turned a divine Labour into work experience. Regardless of whether he received that payment in the end. So, two more Labours are added to the list if Hercules wants to absolve himself of his terrible crimes and to be granted immortality.

11. OBTAINING THE APPLES OF THE HESPERIDES

The Hesperides were three nymphs who guarded a tree of golden apples, in a garden sacred to Hera at the very western edge of the known world. After a long journey across the Mediterranean to find the garden, Hercules encounters Atlas. He is one of the original gods of Greek mythology, who chose the losing side of a great war in the heavens. His punishment from the victor, Zeus, was to be banished to the extremities of the world, where he must hold up the heavens on his back for eternity.

Atlas is often pictured holding up the globe of the earth on his back, and it is for this reason that atlas maps are named after him. But the original tales have him holding up the celestial realm – rather than the earthly realm – for the rest of time. He gives his name to the Atlas Mountains, stretching as they do to the far west world away from Greece, as well as to the Atlantic Ocean and the fictional lost island of Atlantis. Knowing that Atlas is the father of the Hesperides, Hercules realizes this could be his route to stealing the shimmering apples. He grants the god brief respite from his eternal punishment by offering to hold up the heavens for him, in exchange for some golden apples from Atlas' daughters.

Everything seems to go well until Atlas returns with the apples. Unsurprisingly, the god decides he's had enough of holding up the entire heavens, and declares that Hercules can stick at the job himself. Without missing a beat, Hercules agrees – and just asks Atlas to relieve him for a moment so that he can make his cloak more comfortable.

At which point, Hercules makes an inevitable dash, golden apples in hand.

12. CAPTURING CERBERUS

Eurystheus has to come up with one final challenge to Hercules' unstoppable strength, courage and cunning. Only one mission could surely guarantee the hero's death: a trip to the Underworld to capture the mighty Cerberus. He is the vicious three-headed guard dog in the Underworld, and hails from quite some family tree: he is a sibling of the Hydra, as well as of Orthrus, the two-headed guard dog of Geryon's cattle, and is even the uncle of the Nemean Lion. He truly represents the beast of all beasts.

Those who entered the Underworld only did so when they died: no one had ever made a return trip. If through some cunning, Hercules were to make it there and back, surely either the ferocious Cerberus or the wrath of his owner Hades would be the final undoing of the hero. This being the most perilous of all his Labours, Hercules first visits a priest, who conducts rituals to protect him. Hercules climbs down to the Underworld, encountering spirits and monsters along the way, and eventually comes face to face with Hades, the king of the Underworld. Hades gives Hercules permission to take his guard dog – as long as the hero can overpower the beast with his bare hands.

Hercules throws all his strength around Cerberus' three necks, and eventually is able to subdue the creature enough to bring him up to King Eurystheus. Hercules is banished from the Peloponnese, but his Labours are finally over. He is absolved of his terrible crimes and given immortality in life as well as in the stars. Cerberus is returned to Hades unharmed, where he continues to guard the Underworld.

THE MYTH OF HOROSCOPES

Because of the connection of many of Hercules' adventures with constellations, it is possible that the myths were originally created to provide a narrative to the stars that Ancient Greeks saw in the night sky. They saw a crab, a bull and a lion in the twinkling dots above them, and weaved fabulous tales to explain how they got there.

To this day, the power of myth and narrative to explain the inexplicable remains strong. Many people read a daily horoscope or trust in the characteristics of the zodiac signs to make life decisions or choose the right partner. It demonstrates the capacity for stories to help us make sense of the world, even today. In fact, the constellations we associate with modern-day star signs like Aquarius, Taurus and Cancer aren't even in the night sky on the dates we assign to them. The signs of the zodiac, and their dates, were designated a long time ago. The wobbling of the earth in its orbit means that what we see in the night sky evolves over time, in cycles that last nearly 27,000 years. The ancient Romans, Greeks and Babylonians, from whom our zodiac originates, had the constellations in their skies on different dates to when we see the same constellations now.

Astronomically speaking, most of us should truly be the zodiac sign preceding the one we've been assigned. The characteristics of your star sign are therefore not related to the actual stars that were in the sky on your birthdate, but to the stories and myths about the constellations that ancient astrologers saw on different dates in the year. The allure of legends and myths to explain the world will captivate humanity for as long as we can tell stories.

MULAN
CHINESE

The myth of trailblazing heroine Mulan was first written down in about AD 560, but she is believed to have been a Chinese legend for a hundred years or more before that. The first appearance she makes in Chinese literature is in a surprisingly short poem known as the *Ballad of Mulan*. It tells of an utterly distraught young girl, whose father is being called up to join the army, since he has no grown sons to send in his place. Beside herself with worry, Mulan decides that she will go to war in her father's place.

She buys a horse, gets all the gear and dresses herself in men's military robes. She sets out on a journey of thousands of miles to fight in a ten-year war, in which countless warriors lose their life. Eventually, she returns from battle, declines the military honours and rewards that are offered to her, and reveals her true identity.

What you'll read in the story below is a direct translation of the entire original *Ballad of Mulan*. It is an incredibly short poem, which quickly made its way into Chinese folklore. The original lines are in rhythmic, rhyming verse that canters quickly through this extraordinary story. The poem is full of pleasing sounds and onomatopoeic phrases in Chinese that I have tried to capture through the 'rushing and splashing' of the Yellow River, for example. Newer, extended versions of this legend emerged over the centuries, and Mulan reached global recognition with Disney's adaptations in the animated movie of 1999 and the live-action movie of 2020. Every detail in the Disney versions that does not feature in the original text below is an embellishment on the authentic legend. There is no hunky love interest, no national adoration, and no talking dragon. And yet, Disney's interpretations are further examples of folklore in action. Each generation adds its own details and embellishments that feel right for the time that it inhabits.

The emotions that we hear in stories that are hundreds – if not many thousands – of years old are as resonant now as they were millennia ago. The internal conflicts that heroes and heroines face, the fears, love and loss they must endure, and the brave soul-searching they model for us all, are simply part of what it means to be human. This is why the characters that were invented by our ancient ancestors thousands of years ago can readily find themselves animated in a Disney movie. Their emotions, challenges and courage continue to offer answers to humanity's unceasing questions.

THE BALLAD OF MULAN

'No, no!' And again: 'No, no!'

Mulan is weaving in the doorway, and yet we don't hear the slightest noise from the loom shuttle; all we hear is the young girl in terrible torment.

What can she be thinking of? What can she be remembering?

'I'm not thinking about anything! I'm not reminiscing about anything! Last night, I saw the military draft orders – the Khan is rounding up his grand army. There are twelve military scrolls, and roll after roll shows my father's name.

'Oh! My father has no eldest son to send – I have no big brother. Why don't I go to the market and buy a horse and saddle? I could go in my father's place!'

Mulan dashes to the east market for a strong horse, to the west market for a saddle and blanket, to the south market for a bridle, to the north market for a long whip.

At dawn, she departs from her father and mother, and by that evening she rests on the banks of the Yellow River. She doesn't hear the sound of her parents calling out for their daughter, but instead hears the rushing and the splashing of the flowing Yellow River.

The following morning, she leaves the Yellow River behind, and by that evening she reaches the Black Mountain. She doesn't hear the sound of her parents calling out for their daughter, but instead hears the 'Woah!' and the 'Ho!' of the nomadic herders urging their horses.

For ten thousand miles, she goes where the battle takes her, crossing mountain passes as though on wings. The northern winds carry the signal of army gongs, as the reflected frozen light shines off her iron suit.

Generals die after a hundred battles, and after ten long years the heroes journey home. They return to see the divine emperor, sitting in the Bright Hall. There, he bestows a dozen promotions to hundreds of thousands of strong men.

The Khan asks her what she desires. 'I have no need to become one of your officials,' Mulan replies. 'The only thing I desire is the fastest horse that can run a thousand miles to take me back to my hometown.'

Hearing that their daughter is coming home, her parents make their way outside of the city walls, now leaning on each other for support. And now hearing that her little sister is coming home, the elder sister adjusts her make-up in the doorway. Hearing that his big sister is coming home, her little brother grinds his knife sharp and playfully jabs with a swish and a flash in front of the pig and the goat.

'Let me enter the eastern door to my bed chamber, and now sit here on my west-facing bed. I'll take off this military robe, and I'll put on my traditional clothes that I used to wear.'

Standing in the window, Mulan arranges her hair, and now by the mirror applies yellow make-up to her forehead. She steps outside to face her brothers-in-arms. Her comrades are utterly astonished.

'We marched together for twelve long years,' they cry, 'and we had no idea you were a woman!'

Mulan responds: 'The male hare kicks and leaps from left to right, and the female hare has narrower eyes. But when both run side by side along the ground, how can you tell which is male and which is female?'

Chapter 5
Tricksters and Shapeshifters

ricksters and shapeshifters are a mischievous set of characters found in mythology, who often operate outside of the rules and upset the status quo. They can use magical abilities to take on many forms, and they use their cunning and intelligence to outsmart their adversaries and achieve their goals. Tricksters can be both heroic and villainous, and their actions often blur the line between good and evil. They are complex characters who embody both positive and negative traits, and they have the power to both help and hinder humans.

While unpredictable and sometimes violent, these characters feel instantly likeable across many mythologies. Their popularity may be down to their relatability. Their flaws and imperfections make them more human, and their ability to outsmart their opponents using their wit and intelligence is as inspiring as it is entertaining. We love to hear about an underdog outmanoeuvring their opposition, as their victories are seen as a triumph of the human spirit over adversity. The David-and-Goliath moments bring surprise and glee to any listener.

The likeability of tricksters in mythology may also be down to how they provide humour in stories that can often be dark and serious. They are the rebels who challenge authority and power, and we want them to succeed, even if they're not wholly good. They are sometimes portrayed as agents of chaos who disrupt the established order, but who also have the power to restore balance and bring order to the universe. They remind us that there is a delicate balance in the world, and that sometimes it is necessary to upset that balance in order to bring about change and transformation.

THE MONKEY KING
CHINESE

Sun Wukong – the Monkey King – is a violent creature of superhuman strength. He is fiercely intelligent, a cunning trickster, an unpredictable shapeshifter, and an impetuous and proud animal. A significant character in Chinese culture, he features chiefly in the Chinese novel *Journey to the West*, written by Wu Cheng'en in 1592. (He is not to be confused with Hanuman, the monkey king who makes an appearance in the Ancient Indian story of Rama and Sita. See Chapter 5.)

One of the most widely read pieces of literature in East Asia, *Journey to the West* tells of a Buddhist monk known as Tripitaka, who travels from China to India to bring back scriptures to enlighten his people. On his epic journey through forests, over mountains and across deserts, the monk encounters monsters, demons, animal spirits and magical creatures. Some are out to hinder him on his travels, while others become loyal companions.

The Monkey King, Sun Wukong, is one of the characters the monk encounters. Previously the very epitome of cockiness and pride, Sun Wukong was outwitted by Buddha when the monkey's antics had become too much for the gods. Trapped beneath a huge mountain for five hundred years by Buddha, Sun Wukong is finally released when Tripitaka passes by and offers him freedom if the monkey commits to changing his ways. Sun Wukong becomes the first disciple of the monk, but still shows his old ways of violence and trickery. Tripitaka is given a magical gold band by the goddess of mercy, Guanyin. When placed around the monkey's head, Tripitaka is able to tighten it with a chant – keeping the impetuous monkey in check.

Sun Wukong is often depicted with the spoils of his victories: his staff, which can shrink down to the size of a pin or grow to a monolithic bulk, and a golden chainmail suit. He can shapeshift into anything he chooses, and his hairs – when plucked and blown on – can be turned into additional Monkey Kings should the need arise in battle.

In Tripitaka's spiritual journey to enlightenment, Sun Wukong represents the impulsive, violent and reactive part of the human psyche, which must be trained into civility and steadiness. In this way, the Monkey King gradually redeems himself during the novel's one hundred chapters until he reaches true enlightenment.

In the following story, we encounter Sun Wukong

wreaking havoc among the gods. These are some of the acts of trickery that led him to be trapped beneath a mountain for five hundred years before Tripitaka released him.

THE MONKEY KING MEETS
THE DRAGON KING

The ocean moves. Vast columns of water shift to one side, and now to the other side. The waves have been completely parted in two, leaving a dry channel all the way to the seabed, surrounded by the very deepest ocean.

'Give me the finest weapon you have.'

This is how the Old Dragon King of the Eastern Sea is greeted by his visitor, the immortal, unpredictable Monkey King, who now approaches his crystal palace. The Dragon King knows of Sun Wukong's fearsome reputation and is eager not to excite his erratic temper.

'Well, I can offer you this very magical and mighty sword?' the Dragon King suggests, as he signals at his commanders, the Mackerel and the Eel, to present the gigantic blade.

'No, no, no,' the Monkey King replies. 'This little thing won't do. I am the immortal Monkey King, I am the Great Sage, I am equal to any god. I can vanish and reappear, I can run under the sun or moon without a shadow, I can leap to the very heavens and down to the bottom of the sea, I can travel through stone or metal without batting an eyelid. Neither can water drown me nor fire burn me.

'I have trained all my monkeys in the art of warfare to guard our great cave,' Sun Wukong continues. 'But I don't yet have a weapon for myself that is worthy of my divine skills. I've heard of you as my neighbour with the towering crystal palace, and I was sure you'd have some magical weapon befitting of my needs.'

Now beginning to tremble at the thought of provoking the monkey's wrath, the Dragon King sends forth two further commanders, the Bream and the Carp, to heave out a mighty, decorated axe, gigantic in size and protected with celestial powers to ward off spells and protect its bearer from harm.

'Nope. You must have something else. Keep looking.'

THE MONKEY KING FINDS HIS WEAPON

'Well, there is one thing, I suppose,' the Dragon King says doubtfully. 'In the inner depths of my palace is a towering iron staff. It was used to pound out the great Milky Way across the sky, and it is one of the divine iron nails that Yu the Great used to fix the depths of the rivers and seas when he brought all water under control.'

Sun Wukong feels exhilarated by the provenance of this iron staff: 'Excellent. Bring it out.'

'But, but,' the dragon stutters, 'it cannot be moved. You'll have to come and see for yourself. It's been glowing a most intriguing aura for the past few days. I wonder if somehow it has known about your visit.'

They venture deep into the Dragon King's palace, which

seems to grow brighter and brighter the deeper they go. Eventually, they reach the iron staff, now glowing a blinding gold. Sun Wukong runs both hands over its gleaming surface and wraps his arms around the mighty trunk.

'If only it were a bit smaller,' he muses. With that, the staff shimmers and shrinks down to the size of the monkey's palm. 'Ha-ha!' he shrieks out in a deafening laugh. 'Now grow,' Sun Wukong commands, and the staff instantly bulges into a monumental column, nearly taking out the crystal palace's vaulted ceiling. Then he directs it to shrink again – this time to a pin so small that he can hide it inside his ear. Whatever its size, small or monolithic, the monkey leaps about the halls spinning, darting and bounding with his new weapon.

Before leaving the Dragon King, Sun Wukong demands more. He threatens his generous host with his powerful staff, and cajoles him and the Dragon Kings of the north, south and west to fashion him a golden chainmail suit of armour, give him a pair of flying sandals, and offer him a phoenix-winged golden helmet. Incredulous at his ungrateful and violent demands, they soon send word up to heaven about this unpredictable creature.

DEATH COMES CALLING

Sun Wukong returns to his kingdom of monkeys a hero – immortal, powerful and now brandishing a weapon worthy of the very best of the gods. However, the drink-fuelled celebrations that follow are short-lived: in the darkness of the night, the Monkey King is kidnapped by two unknown assailants and dragged deep down, far away from his home. When he comes around from his drunken slumber, he sees that he and his captors are approaching looming, dark city walls, above which is inscribed: *The Land of the Dead*.

'This is King Yuma's Land of the Dead!' Sun Wukong cries out. 'Why have you brought me here?'

The two henchmen shrug their shoulders. 'Your name was on the list,' one of them offers. 'I guess it's your time to die.' And with that, they continue to drag the Monkey King through the towering city gates. With a swift shake, Sun Wukong drops the tiny iron pin from his ear, which grows in an instant into a powerful, whirling staff. The two soldiers are killed by a few swift swipes of the weapon. The monkey bounds through the city, leaping through the streets and across the building tops, spinning and striking his staff, crushing demon soldiers and sending them flying in all directions despite their strength.

CHEATING DEATH

Down in the Underworld sit the Ten Kings in their ten palaces. There they hear the cases of the dead and pass the final judgements. Discovering the chaos that is being wrought in the streets of the Underworld, they look down on the merciless beast that now approaches them.

'I am Sun Wukong,' the Monkey King booms out to them. 'I am equal to any god, and I am immortal. Why have your thugs brought me to this place?'

The Ten Kings scurry about, desperately looking

through their records and registers to see whether there has been a terrible mistake, or whether this truly is the time for Sun Wukong to leave the world of the living. They hunt through the scrolls for running animals, hairy animals, flying animals, hairless animals, humans and more. Nowhere is his name to be found. But then, there it is, in the register for monkeys: Sun Wukong, destined to enter the Land of the Dead.

The Monkey King will not accept this. He grabs the scroll from the Ten Kings, snatches a paintbrush and crosses out his name with a big smudge – and every other name from the list of monkeys. He stares death's own judges in the eyes one by one: 'We're done here,' he utters, and flings the scroll to the floor. He swings his way back through the city of death, bludgeoning demons as he makes his way back to the world of the living.

The judges of the Underworld sit terrified until the vicious visitor has gone. Only then do they send a report to the gods of the dreadful things this creature has done – a report that starts to build to litany of contemptuous crimes. It is said that you will never see a monkey in old age to this day, because the Monkey King cheated death for all of his kingdom.

ANANSI
GHANAIAN AND CARIBBEAN

Anansi is a mythical creature that originated among the Akan people of West Africa, in what is modern-day Ghana and Ivory Coast, where his name means *Spider*.

Anansi is often portrayed as a trickster figure, known for his cleverness, cunning and his ability to shapeshift into spider- and human-like forms. The many legends of Anansi see him outwitting other creatures and humans, using his intelligence and plotting to achieve his goals.

His popularity spread to other countries in Africa, and eventually across to the Caribbean with the trade of enslaved African people. The significance of myth and storytelling to unite displaced people cannot be understated. Sharing stories from one person to another remains one of the few ways to preserve a shared history, a culture under threat and a personal sense of identity.

In the Caribbean, Anansi is a symbol of resistance against oppression. His cunning and intelligence were interpreted as a way for enslaved people to resist their oppressors. It is said that his stories were used as a way to pass on important information, such as escape plans, while remaining undetected by slave owners.

As the stories have been passed down from person to person, there seem to be as many versions of Anansi's myths as there are ears to hear them. He continues to be a popular figure in folklore and children's stories, as his tales are not only entertaining but serve as a teaching tool. His popularity across oceans and generations demonstrates how one spider can cast a web around the world.

THE KEEPER OF ALL STORIES

A long, long time ago, all the stories belonged to the sky god Nyame. The people of earth had no myths to tell, no knowledge to share, and no campfire tales to explain the world around them.

The cunning, shapeshifting Anansi has a problem with this. He wants humanity to know about its history and he wants to share the stories that help mankind define who they are. He shoots a web up to the heavens, confidently marches up to the gigantic form of Nyame, and tells him of his important plan.

'I've come to take all the stories to the people of earth,' Anansi proclaims. 'I want them to understand who they are, and where they come from.'

The sky god booms laughter across the sky like thunder.

'Can this tiny spider be earnest in his challenge of such a mighty god?' roars Nyame. 'Many powerful kings have come before me with a similar request to take away my stories, and none has been able to pay the worth of all of the stories of the world.'

'Name your price!' Anansi offers. 'I will pay anything.'

Nyame considers this, and smirks. He agrees that Anansi can have the stories – but on one condition: he must bring to the god the four most ferocious beasts on earth.

'Bring me Onini the python, bring me Osebo the leopard, bring me the Mmoboro hornets, and bring me Mmoatia the forest spirit. Only then can you have all the stories.' Nyame chuckles to himself, confident that little Anansi has no hope of completing this impossible task.

'Right you are!' comes the spider's undaunted response,

and he immediately turns on his eight heels and heads back down to the land. His cunning mind is already weaving a plan.

ONINI THE PYTHON

His first target is the python Onini. Anansi takes his wife, Aso, as his accomplice for this first treacherous task. When they reach Onini's land, the two spiders start an argument with one another, just loud enough to be sure that the snake will hear. Coiled around the vast, thick branch of a tree and resting in the sun, Onini is suddenly awoken. He opens one eye and eavesdrops on the arachnids' quarrel.

'No, no, no. He's definitely shorter than this bamboo cane,' Aso insists, vociferously. 'They say Onini is the longest animal that has ever existed, but I don't believe it. I bet he's not even as big a this bit of bamboo.'

She glances up at the gigantic python's resting place to see if he will take the bait. Now fully awake, Onini is outraged by such insolence from these tiny creatures. He slithers over to the bamboo pole and stretches himself along it to prove he is indeed far longer than anything else on earth.

'See!' insists the snake. 'Just as I suspected. This silly stick is significantly smaller than my stretched-out scales!'

While Onini is comparing himself to the bamboo pole, Anansi and Aso rush in and bind him to the stick with creeping vines. They wrap their webs around him and, before the great python knows what has happened, he is strapped up and unable to move. The delighted spiders never doubted their success, and they happily present the great beast to Nyame.

The sky god is somewhat surprised, but reminds Anansi that he has three more creatures to capture if he has any hope of becoming the Keeper of All Stories.

OSEBO THE LEOPARD

Anansi knows that overpowering the great leopard Osebo will be impossible for a tiny spider. The leopard is known for his strength, his violent claws and his terrifyingly sharp teeth that glisten with blood. If he wants to capture such a ferocious beast, he is going to have to use his masterful mind.

Anansi watches the leopard for a few days, and begins to learn his routines and movements. The first thing Osebo does each morning is to take a stroll in the early rays of the sun, down to the waterhole to quench his thirst. The cunning spider digs a huge hole in the dusty ground, and covers it with thin sticks and large palm leaves. He adds a layer of dried leaves and smaller sticks, before dusting it over with some of the earth. The trap is set.

The following morning, Osebo walks sleepily along his route towards the waterhole, and falls right into Anansi's snare. He tumbles one paw after the other through the thin leaves and lands with a thump at the bottom of the deep pit. The leopard tries in vain to get himself up over the vertical walls, using his tremendous claws to dig into the dirt.

'Everything okay down there?' comes a little voice from above.

Anansi offers to help. He weaves a slim, sticky thread down into the leopard's ditch. Osebo paws at the silk as the spider keeps spinning more and more gluey silk.

'Keep grabbing at it!' Anansi advises.

Osebo is so desperate to find a way out of the hole that he does as the spider suggests. The more thread that comes down, the more the leopard grasps at it, entangling his paws, coiling his body as he twists and turns, until he is almost completely entwined in the clever spider's web.

Nyame can't help but be secretly impressed as Anansi presents him with the massive, immobile cat.

THE MMOBORO HORNETS

As Anansi approaches the home of the Mmoboro hornets, the noise of their buzzing grows heavy. They swarm around their hive high up in a towering tree, forming a dark, pulsating cloud of humming. Each insect flashes dangerously in yellow and black as it busies itself in the deafening cacophony, and Anansi can see that any one of them could easily kill him.

The spider finds a hollow gourd near the hornets' tree, which he fills with water from a nearby pond. He carries the heavy vessel up to the very top branches, and begins his deceit. He trickles the water from the gourd out over the entire tree, drenching the leaves, the boughs and eventually the hornets' hive itself. Anansi runs down the trunk of the tree on his eight legs until he reaches the unhappy hornets.

'Quick!' he yells. 'It's raining! Don't stay out here and

risk the death of the whole colony. Your hive is already getting saturated.'

His wise words have caught the attention of the queen.

'Come here – I have shelter,' the spider offers. He points with as many hands as he can to the hollow gourd, which now looks very dry and inviting on the inside. The queen sees the opportunity and climbs through the narrow opening at the top of the vast vegetable.

The rest of the hornets needs no encouragement. Where one goes, they all go! With the chaotic buzz of a thousand motors, the hornets swarm the gourd, crawling and teeming and squeezing through the narrow neck until every last insect is inside. Anansi plugs the top of the vegetable, and almost skips his way up to Nyame with his third offering.

MMOATIA THE FOREST SPIRIT

The final challenge for Anansi looks like the most demanding of all. He has been able to use the python's length to bind up Onini, he has used the leopard's grabbing paws to entwine Osebo, and he has used the hornet's swarming impulse to capture the Mmoboro Hornets; but now he has to outsmart Mmoatia, a strong-willed spirit of the forest. Anansi travels deep into the dark forest until he reaches a magical odum tree, where the spirits live. If he is to capture this woodland fairy, he has to appeal to her strong emotions. This is his most elaborate plan so far.

First, he carves a wooden Akua doll, the size of an ordinary small girl. Then, he gathers the sticky sap that is oozing out from the trunk of a gum tree, and covers the doll in the tacky goo. Next, he makes a bowl of delicious yam mash – a favourite dish of the forest spirits – and he lays it before his doll, right by the odum tree. Finally, he spins some of his silky threads to the doll's body, and holds on to them from his hiding place on the other side of the tree's trunk.

After a short wait, Mmoatia comes by the odum tree. Her first instinct is to notice the irresistible bowl of yam mash. Only then does she see the young girl sitting by it. The food looks so heavenly that she asks the girl if she could possibly try some of her meal.

Silence.

The doll doesn't say a word, and ignores Mmoatia completely. This is outrageous! How dare she ignore this beautiful forest spirit, who has asked so nicely to have some of her delicious food?

Mmoatia stamps her feet and screams, 'Why are you ignoring me?!'

With that, she slaps the doll round the face in utter indignation. But her hand sticks to the silly doll's face. Mmoatia can't move it. She lashes out with the other hand to smack this insolent girl, and her other hand sticks fast to the doll's body. Now panicking, she kicks and screams and rolls around, with each movement attaching herself ever more to the sticky sap.

Once the forest spirit can fight no more, Anansi pulls at the threads and drags Mmoatia up to the sky god as his final offering.

NYAME HANDS OVER THE STORIES

Nyame is unable to deny the cunning of Anansi's trickery. The clever spider used the snake's length as the weapon to catch Onini, the leopard's strength to enmesh Osebo, the hive's swarming instinct to entrap the Mmoboro hornets, and finally the forest spirit's pride and anger to deceive Mmoatia.

Nyame begrudgingly honours his deal, and entrusts Anansi with all of the world's stories. The spider is bestowed the great honour of becoming the Keeper of All Stories, and he shares all the legends and myths from the dawn of time among humanity. The people of earth finally have a way to understand where they have come from, to rejoice in their shared identity, and to understand important lessons through the stories they are able to tell.

STORIES BIGGER THAN OURSELVES

In several ancient civilizations, the myths that are told are thought to be more than just manmade stories; they are said to come from the gods themselves. The Dreaming of Australia's First Nations (see Chapter 1), the Ten Commandments bestowed to Moses in the Christian Bible, and the holy text itself of the Qur'an and other religious books, all claim to come from something beyond humanity. Likewise, Anansi gifts the art of storytelling to humankind, giving the tales themselves a celestial origin and a sense of momentous eternity.

They aren't just stories about animals and gods and stars

and floods and journeys and love and death. Somehow, these legends are universal. They talk about guiding principles that are bigger than any one person, and bigger in fact than all people.

Because they have been passed down from one campfire narrator to the next for countless generations, they do indeed exist somewhere in the narrative of the human race itself. They are from a place outside of standard chronology. They have always existed and will continue to do so for as long as humankind will have ideas to share.

Chapter 6

Nature

ature has inspired many of the greatest stories told. It is understandable that the sheer scale of the vast mountains, plunging valleys and towering islands of the natural landscape moved our ancient ancestors to question what giant powers must have formed them. The unstoppable forces that they witnessed nature unleashing on the world drove them to query who might be in control of it all.

Across the planet and across thousands of years, each civilization conceived its own myths to gain their own sense of control over the unpredictable. Floods, storms, famine, volcanoes and earthquakes all became rich ground upon which to base their legends and religions. The Māori people had Tangaroa, god of the ocean and father of the fish. He would be the one to decree the power of the sea and the bounty of the fishermen's nets. The Ancient Greeks had Poseidon, the sea god pulled by the white horses of the breaking waves. With one strike of his vast trident on the sea floor, he could conjure tidal waves and storms that would blow whole army fleets off course. For the K'iche' Mayan people, the sun made its course across the huge arc of the sky in the mouth of Q'uq'umatz, the Sovereign Plumed Serpent. (See more about the K'iche' Mayan origin story in Chapter 1: *Popol Vuh*.)

In creating such gods and spirits, ancient civilizations were able to imagine the almost inconceivable powers that were needed to create the landscapes, oceans, natural disasters and cosmology that they could see. In this chapter, you'll hear about the lovable demigod Māui of the Māori people and how he created the vast islands of New Zealand in the middle of the wide ocean, and about the incredibly emotional origin of the changing seasons, according to the Ancient Greeks.

MĀUI
MĀORI

Māui is the shapeshifting demigod of Polynesian mythology, which covers many of the thousand islands scattered across the Central and South Pacific Ocean. Over centuries from about 1300 BC, the Polynesian people migrated across the vast expanses of ocean from Fiji and Samoa to the Cook Islands, down to New Zealand and across as far as Easter Island to the east and Hawai'i to the north. As each bold set of pioneers sailed and rowed towards their new lands, they stowed away stories, legends and folklore in their canoes with them.

In this way, the tales of Māui and his adventures have become intertwined in Polynesian legend, spread across 6,000 kilometres of ocean. His role in Pacific oral tradition is essential in understanding the relationship of its people with the sea and with their shared ancestry. Through his many feats, such as pulling up islands from the depths of the sea and slowing down the path of the sun, Māui not only serves as an example of strength and daring, but also symbolizes the power of ingenuity, exploration and innovation that the Polynesian people brought with them on their heroic migrations.

This story follows the Māori tradition of Aotearoa, the traditional name for New Zealand, and is an example of myth being used to explain extraordinary geographical features – such as islands in the middle of a vast ocean with nothing in sight around them other than water. Very similar versions of this legend have also been portrayed as the origins for both the Tongan and Hawai'ian islands, one of which bears Māui's name, as do traditional names for New Zealand's North and South Islands.

A FISHING TRIP

Māui's brothers are heading out for a fishing trip once again, and they refuse to take him, mocking him for being too young, too inexperienced and too weak. He grows increasingly jealous of their canoe adventures across the cyan blue ocean, spending their days far out in the warm sea breezes and salty air. So, enraged, the cunning Māui comes up with a plan to get himself out into the ocean with his brothers.

Before sunrise the following morning, he takes the jawbone fishing hook gifted to him by his grandmother, the great goddess Muri-ranga-whenua. Praying for protection and guidance through this magical hook, he binds it with a strong fishing line. The sky floods with the pink and orange dawn as Māui's brothers ready their canoe – known as a *waka* – and they don't see the mischievous boy conceal himself in a basket at the back.

The four men row the *waka* out from the shore, striking the deep water with their oars in unison to head out to a distant fishing spot. Once there, it doesn't take them long to discover the rascal hiding on board.

'What are you doing here, Māui?' the oldest brother shouts. 'This is no place for a little boy like you. We are way out to sea now, so just sit there and don't touch anything.'

'I'll catch the biggest fish of all – you just wait!' boasts Māui. His brothers all stare at him with blank expressions before roaring with laughter and slapping each other on the arms at the little boy's delusion. They refuse to give him any bait, and tell him to sit tight while they get on with the real work. But they don't know about Māui's magical fishing hook.

MĀUI'S CATCH

Undeterred by his brothers' obstinance, the young boy pricks his finger with the sharp hook. He winces as it draws blood – this will be his bait. Māui swings the jawbone hook around his head and casts it far into the turquoise waves. The others roll their eyes at first, but soon notice something very unusual is happening. The hook sinks deep down to the ocean floor, held fast by the extraordinarily firm fishing line that Māui has woven.

Unbelievably, the hook finds a bite. The brothers look on in amazement as Māui pulls and struggles with all of his might against what must be a colossus of a catch. Overwhelmed and terrified by the frothing ocean, the men plead with the young boy to let go of whatever has taken his bait. They can make out a vast, dark shape lifting from the very depths beneath the chopping, blue waves.

Māui wants to prove to his brothers that he is a worthy fisherman, and he calls for them all to grab hold of the fishing line. They pull with every last breath of strength in their bodies, as the gigantic shadow in the water grows larger and larger. Just as they think they can give no more effort, the catch starts to emerge from the churning waves, and the gigantic shape keeps on growing.

'Look at my fish!' Māui squeals. 'It's as big as an island!'

And indeed it is now the fish-shaped North Island in Aotearoa, known as Te Ika-a-Māui – or *the fish of Māui*. And their canoe is commemorated in the long shape of the South Island, known by some as Te Waka a Māui – or *the canoe of Māui*.

Māui pleads with his brothers not to chop up the fish until he has offered a prayer in blessing for this miraculous catch, but the impatient men won't listen to the little rascal. They chop and cut and slice at the fish greedily, which is why the land is so ragged with mountains, plains, ravines and cliffs. Had they waited, the island would still retain its perfect fish shape.

THE SIGNIFICANCE IN A NECKLACE

One of the most recognized Māori symbols worn by many today is the jawbone fishhook necklace. Originally a practical tool worn by fishermen, the modern equivalent is a decorative version made in a variety of materials. Known as a *hei matau*, the necklace is often associated with the tale of Māui and the inception of the Aotearoa islands. What may at first seem like a simple necklace worn by locals and tourists alike is, in fact, a deeply meaningful symbol of the dawn of New Zealand, born from the ocean intermingled with the demigod's own blood.

PERSEPHONE AND HADES
GREEK

The Greek pantheon is possibly one of the most widely recognized across the world. It has given us bearded Zeus with his thunderbolt spear, trident-carrying Poseidon of the sea, arrow-wielding Eros firing love into the hearts of humanity, sandal-winged messenger god Hermes and the goddess of love Aphrodite. It was so admired in the ancient world of the Mediterranean that the Romans readily assimilated the Greek deities into their own pantheon, often embellishing and improving on the myths handed down by the Greeks to make them better reflect Roman ideals. Many of the same stories of those Greek gods were changed into Roman legends, giving them more Roman-sounding names in most cases. Zeus became thunder-crashing Jupiter, Poseidon became the sea god Neptune, Eros handed his arrows over to the Roman version Cupid, the messenger god was renamed Mercury, and the goddess of love became Venus.

This Greek story of Persephone, abducted by god of the Underworld Hades, comes from a series of thirty-three very ancient Greek poems known as the *Homeric Hymns*. You can read more about Homer in Chapter 10, under *The Odyssey*, where you will discover that the famous poet probably didn't write any of the works that are attributed to him. In fact, there is no real suggestion that he had anything to do with the *Homeric Hymns* either – other than the fact that the rhythmic style of the poetry is the same. Composed sometime around the sixth century BC, this story of Persephone was committed to writing only a few generations after the Greek writing system was invented. It truly is one of the oldest stories in existence, and was used by Greeks and Romans alike to explain the harshness of famine and changeability of the seasons.

PERSEPHONE IS ABDUCTED

A horrendous scream resounds up to the heavens. The olive trees shake and the mountains tremble with Persephone's call out to her father Zeus. And yet her cries are heard by no one other than the nymph Sion, who saw her friend disappear from the meadow. She saw how Persephone was entranced by an utterly bewitching narcissus flower and how, as she leant down to pick it up, the ground opened up to reveal the dark god of the Underworld himself. She saw how Hades grabbed the powerless Persephone, threw her into the back of his golden chariot and cracked the whip for his shadowy horses to fly away at speed. At that sight, Sion wept so much for her friend that she created a vast pool of water that flowed to become the River Sion.

Zeus is deaf to the screams that call his name now – perhaps because it was he who placed that entrancing flower for his defenceless daughter to find. He rules the heavens, and his brother Hades rules the Underworld. Hades is in love with the girl, but he knows that no mother would approve of their daughter marrying the king of the dead, and so Zeus has had to get involved. Zeus made sure that the enticing narcissus sprouted away from the other nymphs, to lure Persephone to a spot where Hades could abduct the unwitting girl.

DEMETER IS GRIEF-STRICKEN

The goddess of the rich harvest and fertile crops is beside herself. As Persephone's mother, Demeter searches across the land for her daughter. The people of earth see Demeter's pain and know they must do something to preserve her good nature. She has shown them the skill of agriculture and provides them with food and vegetation, and they must pay their deep respects for what she yields. A vast temple is built in the goddess's name, where prayers and sacrifices are made to bring about bountiful harvests across the earth. But Demeter is inconsolable. She sits in that temple and hides away from the other gods, wasting away as she laments her darling daughter.

In Demeter's grief, the earth suffers: no seed sprouts from the ground, despite the efforts of humankind. They heave their oxen to plough their fields and exert themselves to sow grain, but all for nothing. The earth becomes barren and sparse, and it gets so bad that Zeus has to step in, sending god after god to coax Demeter from her isolation. Nothing will work, as all she wants to do is to see her daughter Persephone again.

A VISIT TO THE UNDERWORLD

Zeus finally relents and sends the messenger god Hermes down to the Underworld to convince the dark lord to release his bride; this will be the only way to save the mortal humans from their deadly famine.

'Hades, king of the dead!' Hermes calls out when he reaches the dark realm of the Underworld. 'The great king of the gods, Zeus himself, has ordered that Persephone returns to the heavens to be with her mother, so she may see her with her own eyes. Demeter's grief has caused a terrible famine killing off entire cities of mortals – she is destroying the honour they have for all of the gods. It will be bad news for us all without their respect.'

Hades raises his dark brows and leans over to his wife. 'Persephone,' he says, 'go to your mother. I'm your husband and I love you, so don't be upset. Whenever you stay in the Underworld you will be queen of it all, and you will have all the prayers and worship of the living and the dead. But go to your mother – she needs you now.'

Hermes is surprised by the dark god's respect and compassion, and by how Persephone appears to be a content, divine queen of his realm. He doesn't notice, therefore, when Hades gives Persephone six pomegranate seeds to eat, to signify his ownership of her down in the Underworld. Once she eats from his food, she belongs to the land of the dead.

A COMPROMISE IS AGREED

Persephone travels in Hades' golden chariot pulled by his immortal horses, this time a joyful journey from the Underworld over land and sea until she reaches her mother. Demeter can't believe the sight of her daughter approaching, and springs from her isolation in the temple down the mountainside to embrace Persephone. Demeter's mood lifts and, almost instantly, verdant and fertile vegetation flourishes over the earth. Mother and daughter are reunited, and they reconcile with the other gods on Mount Olympus. Conscious of his brother Hades having been left without his bride in the Underworld, Zeus asks his daughter where she would like to live. It is clear that the fruit from Hades' hand has sealed their bond.

'Hades has been really kind to me,' Persephone tells her father. 'I really want to be by my husband's side.'

After such abject grief, Demeter can barely contain her rage. Darkness surrounds her, and Zeus realizes he must reach a compromise before the world is starved again.

'Here is what will happen,' the father of the gods decrees. 'Persephone spends half the year down in the Underworld with her husband Hades, and half the year up here with her mother.'

Seeing how happy her daughter appears, Demeter realizes that she has no option but to agree to this compromise. Her grief, however, does not change as the years go by. And so it is that for half the year, Demeter still withholds growth and plenty from the earth, no matter how much effort humankind puts into its fields, but for the other half of the year when Demeter is reunited with her daughter, there is fertile growth across the world. Demeter teaches humanity the proper rituals and prayers to honour the life-giving riches she bestows on the earth, and only those who conduct these rites will be able to feed in the Underworld after they have died.

Chapter 7
Love

ove has inspired the greatest stories ever told. It is possibly the strongest emotion that humans can feel, and certainly one of the biggest drivers of our actions. It makes us do irrational things, it brings us to the extremes of our feeling, and inspires us to travel the earth – and sometimes even into the Underworld – to be with the person of our adoration.

However, to love is to live in fear of losing that love.

Stories about love – both ancient and modern – come hand in hand with stories about loss and grief. The myths in this chapter are inextricably bound to death and heartbreak. It is a tumultuous and unpredictable force in humanity, and therefore features heavily in the stories we tell. There is no Hollywood or Bollywood movie that doesn't have a turbulent love story at its heart. And narrators of ancient legends were just as consumed by the topic.

Having said that, ancient mythologies do sometimes treat the matter of love differently to how we would expect in modern movies. In most ancient civilizations, marriage was a thing that men did to women, rather than a mutual agreement between two lovers. Sometimes, the matter-of-fact approach to marriage in myths can make them feel cold to our modern ears. However, what remains unchanged over millennia of storytelling is the strength of feeling that comes from one person loving another. And the loss of that love brought our ancestors to tears thousands of years ago in exactly the same way it does today.

Love stories can inspire great joy and passion, but they can also portray abject heartbreak and tragedy. Love is a force that is both powerful and fragile, capable of bringing people together or tearing them apart.

PYRAMUS AND THISBE
ROMAN

The greatest love stories ever told inevitably blend passion with tragedy and loss. The myth of two lovers, Pyramus and Thisbe, is retold in Roman poet Ovid's *Metamorphoses*. This phenomenal poem from AD 8 catalogues over two hundred and fifty different myths from the dawn of time, all the way up to the deification of Julius Caesar. As the title suggests, Ovid's legends are about change and transformation. The heroes in each of his tales often meet a grisly end and are mutated into a landscape feature, a constellation, a unique plant, or an animal. He uses vivid mythological tales to explain the origins of the natural world around us.

This story tells of the ill-fated romance between Pyramus, a handsome young man, and Thisbe, his beautiful neighbour. Despite the fact that their families are bitter rivals, Pyramus and Thisbe fall deeply in love and decide to run away together. Fans of Shakespeare will notice more than a few similarities between this short tale and the tragedy of *Romeo and Juliet*. Both stories feature young lovers who are forced to flee their families to pursue their love, and both end in tragic deaths caused by a misunderstanding in the final moments of life. Shakespeare doesn't hide the fact that he is a fan of Ovid's story; he even satirizes the tale of Pyramus and Thisbe in a comic scene in his play *A Midsummer Night's Dream*.

In the end, Ovid uses their gruesome deaths as the origin story for why the fruits of the mulberry tree turn from white to pink and purple as they ripen. It is a beautiful and heart-rending myth that many Romans would have retold as they bit into a blood-red mulberry pie.

TWO HOUSEHOLDS, BOTH ALIKE IN DIGNITY

Pyramus is undeniably a handsome young man, but everyone across Babylonia speaks of Thisbe as the most understatedly beautiful girl. Their families live side by side in the walled city of Assyria, so close that the young pair met as soon as they could walk. As they grow, so does their affection for one another – and now they would marry if only their fathers weren't so staunchly against the idea.

Their parents can forbid a marriage, but they cannot forbid the love that burns between these two likeminded spirits. Although they can't speak openly, the lovers communicate through a lingered glance, a knowing nod, a shared, private smile. The more their fathers suppress the glowing embers of their love, the more intensely the heat burns between them.

There is just one wall that separates their two homes, and in one corner is a narrow crack. It has gone unnoticed for centuries, but love finds every opportunity. The couple start to meet by the wall that divides them. Their gentle, murmured words carry from one side to the other and back again, reaching where physical caresses cannot.

Thisbe often sits this side, and Pyramus on the other, feeling the whispering breath pass between their lips.

'Damn this wall!' they frequently say. 'Why are you blocking our love? Even if we can't be together, can't we at least share one kiss?'

Each night, they sit together but isolated, and whisper their vain hopes before a final goodnight. The lovers blow a kiss each way, neither of which reaches the other.

They need to get away.

One night, they devise a desperate plan. Under the cover of darkness the following night, they will slip past their parents, they will leave their homes and the city walls behind them. They will meet at the tomb of King Ninus, where they can remain unseen beneath a tall mulberry tree, overladen with snow-white berries.

The next day feels endless to the impatient lovers. The sun rises and seems to take an eternity to drift its path across the vast sky. Separately, they watch it arc high over the land and eventually – finally! – sink slowly into the sea, from where dusk now spreads.

It is time.

Thisbe covers her face with a veil, quietly opens the gate, and slips out into the shadows, unnoticed by her parents. Catching her breath for the first time, she reaches the tomb. She lets out a laugh and settles beneath the mulberry tree. Love certainly has made her bold.

Just at that moment, she notices something approach through the moonlight. Could it be? The unmistakable shoulders of a fully grown lioness undulate as it walks towards the nearby spring to quench its thirst. The moon is bright, and Thisbe can see the lioness's jaws frothing red with the blood of slaughtered oxen.

She freezes. Catching herself again, her hands start to tremble. Thisbe tries not to make a sound as she makes a dash towards the shelter of a dark cave a little way from the tree. In her haste, her veil slips from her shoulders and floats serenely to the ground in the glistening light of the moon. She doesn't dare to pause and pick it up, instead thinking only of her hiding place in the cave.

The lioness has drunk its full from the spring and now prowls back towards the forest. As it passes the mulberry tree, the bloodthirsty creature sniffs at the white veil on the ground, and angrily tears at it with its bloody jaws before moving on beyond the dark treeline. Thisbe is lucky to escape unseen by the beast.

Just a moment later, Pyramus arrives at the lovers' meeting point. Approaching the tomb, he squints to make out the unmistakable footprints of a large lion in the dusty ground. His face turns as pale as the moonlight.

Jittery with fear, he rounds the mulberry tree. His breath leaves him when he sees on the ground Thisbe's white veil, shredded and covered in dark red blood.

'What have I done?' he cries out into the night. 'I've killed you! My love! I made you come out here in the dark by yourself – I should have come here first.'

Pyramus is beside himself with guilt: 'Where is that lion? Come and tear me apart as well! Rip out my entrails with your cruel jaws! I deserve to die.'

He picks up the veil and kisses it repeatedly, as his tears mix with the blood.

'My kisses and tears are yours. Here – have my blood as well.'

He presses the cold steel of his sword into his side and slides it deep into his bowels.

As he pulls out the blade, the world swims around his head, and he falls to the ground. Bright red blood gushes out of his wound like the hissing jet of a broken water pipe. The ground is so drenched that the thousands of white berries on the heavy branches grow purple with the blood soaked up from the earth.

Leaving her cave, Thisbe brushes herself off from her scare with the lioness and makes her way back towards the tomb. Her darling lover must be waiting for her. She can't wait to tell him about her brave escape, and looks around for him with increasing concern.

The berries are red, and her face grows white.

In terrifying disbelief, she sees his wounded body beneath the tree, covered in blood. She stumbles backwards, shuddering like the sea when it is brushed by a cold breeze. She knows this is her beloved Pyramus – she cannot deny it. In a frenzy, she pulls at her hair, scratches her arms and utters incomprehensible laments into the night air.

Thisbe's arms grab at Pyramus' body on the ground, trying in vain to lift up her lover. Grief runs down her face and soaks his wounds. She kisses his cold and bloody lips, and through her uncontrollable sobbing she calls out to him: 'Pyramus! Pyramus! Wake up! Please get up. It's me – Thisbe.'

At Thisbe's name, Pyramus lifts his heavy eyelids. His eyes roll as the darkness of death hovers around him.

He sees the veil on the ground. He sees his ivory sheath nearby – but not his sword.

Thisbe continues to call out: 'You've died by your love for me and by your own hand. And me? Will my hand be as bold as yours? My love will do the deed. Death cannot separate us.

'And to our poor parents, I ask you to hear our misery. We are now united in our eternal love and endless death, and I pray you don't deny us a shared tomb.'

She looks up to the red boughs of the mulberry tree above them. 'And this tree, you spread your gloomy shadows on one body, and soon will on another. Grieve our deaths, and let your berries darken in the memory of our blood.'

Thisbe says no more. She positions the sword beneath her breast and falls down onto the blade, even now still warm with Pyramus' blood.

Her prayers reached the gods, and they reached their parents. The mulberries now darken as they ripen on the branch in memory of the couple, and the ashes of the tragic pair rest together in one urn.

AENEAS AND DIDO
ROMAN

The greatest love stories ever told are never far removed from the greatest tragedies. Our second love story, that of Aeneas and Dido, returns to a heart-breaking theme of betrayal and loss. Composed in the first century BC by Roman poet Virgil, *The Aeneid* is an epic tale of the hero Aeneas. He is a hero of Troy, an ancient city located on the Aegean coast of modern-day Turkey. He was related to Troy's king, descended from Troy's founding father, and was the son of the goddess of love herself, Venus. The city of Troy features heavily in Greek literature, mythology and theatre, often focusing on the mythical ten-year War of Troy, when the city was eventually conquered by the attacking Greek armies.

The Romans idolized Greek literature, art and stories, and borrowed heavily from all aspects of Greek culture. The baton that the Greeks held in architecture, law, academia, literature, technology and beyond was gladly snatched up by the Romans and improved upon. They would have read texts from Greek philosophers like Plato and Aristotle, and from Greek poetry such as Homer's *Odyssey* and *Iliad*. Aeneas' role in Greek literature is minimal, but he truly gets his time in the spotlight after Virgil was commissioned to write Rome's own versions of Homer's epic tales.

Rome's first emperor, Augustus Caesar, came to power after decades of political unrest, culminating in the assassination of his adopted father, Julius Caesar.

Augustus expanded the Roman Empire in all directions, annexing land and people in modern-day Spain, Portugal, Switzerland, Germany, Austria, Slovenia, Hungary, Israel, Tunisia, Libya and beyond. Understandably, he was keen to inject some much-needed stability into the ever-growing population, and to get new nations on board with his vision of what it meant to be Roman. This is where Virgil came in, to create a new version of Rome's origin story, by using very ancient influences from Greek legends that would have been familiar to the Roman audience.

Aeneas' beloved city of Troy is finally sacked by the Greeks, and he is given the divine mission to set out on an epic voyage across the Mediterranean Sea to find a new land for his people, and to establish the eternal city of Rome. That will be the site of a great civilization. Broadly speaking, the first six books of Virgil's *Aeneid* share similarities with Homer's *Odyssey*, in that they follow a hero who must make an adventurous journey through weird and wonderful lands. He encounters gods, monsters and guides along the way, and must overcome challenges in order to continue on his profound duty to found the city of Rome. The second six books of *The Aeneid* share similarities with Homer's battle-heavy *Iliad*, as Aeneas arrives on Italian soil and wages war with the locals before the Roman civilization is born.

The following love story takes place as Aeneas travels the sea and land towards his destiny. Along his legendary journey, he and his ships land in Carthage on the northern coast of modern-day Tunisia. There he meets the recently widowed Queen Dido, and the gods see an opportunity to meddle in the hero's voyage. In this translation from

Virgil's *Aeneid*, we join the story as Aeneas has finished recounting to his host brave and tragic tales of the ten-year War of Troy. (You can discover more about Aeneas' heroic tales on page 129: The Trojan Horse.)

DIDO IS SMITTEN BY AENEAS' STORIES

A fire burns in Carthage. No longer are the embers in the palace hearth glowing, but it is the flames in Queen Dido's heart that are dancing giddily. She has spent another evening listening to the utterly incredible stories of her mysterious and courageous guest. Aeneas' heroic ordeals in the hard-fought War of Troy, together with the adventure and danger of his journey to found a new civilization, have captured Dido's mind. Her guests are long asleep, yet her mind races and returns again and again to the words from Aeneas' lips, to the form of his arms as he rested on the couch, and to the alluring fearlessness of his stories.

Dido is like a deer that darts aimlessly through the forest, not realizing it has been pierced by a hunter's arrow in its flank. At night, she finds herself sitting in the couch where he sat, and during the day, she takes his son Ascanius on her knee; anything to feel closer to this new, enigmatic man. She imagines that her own city of Carthage could join with this Trojan leader to become the powerful civilization he has been selected to found. Dido does not realize she has Cupid's own fatal arrow stuck in her side as she gives in to her love.

THE GODS INTERVENE

From Mount Olympus, queen of the heavens Juno watches the infatuation that is growing in Dido's heart. Juno is an obstacle to Aeneas' mission: she's never been a fan of his mother Venus, and is paranoid about a prophecy that the goddess's sacred city of Carthage will one day be destroyed by descendants of the city of Troy. For this reason, she has kept a watchful eye on Aeneas' progress and hindered him at every step. Now, seeing the queen's fatal attraction to him, and recognizing that he is close to taking the throne next to Dido, Juno decides something must be done. She corners Venus, goddess of love, mother of Aeneas, and Juno's arch rival.

'Oh, lovely Venus,' Juno starts. 'You and your boy Aeneas have done so well after all that terrible business in Troy. And look – he's found his way to my city of Carthage!' Venus eyes Juno suspiciously, who quickly continues. 'Anyway, Dido seems to be utterly infatuated with the boy, and the madness of love is tearing through her veins. Why don't we put aside our petty squabble, and make peace? What good can come from us continuing to fight and cause such chaos on the world below? Let's rule over these people equally – she can take this Trojan as a husband, and you can have the Carthaginians as her dowry.'

Venus can't quite imagine that Jupiter's divine plan for Aeneas to found the new civilization of Rome could simply be switched over for Carthage like this, and she's cautious about Juno's true intentions. Nonetheless, the two goddesses devise a plan that cannot fail to bring the pair closer together.

THE HUNT BEGINS

Dawn's pink light floods Carthage the following morning, and an immense hunt is planned. Dido's horse, decked out in purple and gold, stands bristling with anticipation for the queen, who emerges with her lively entourage, dressed in the most exquisite purple robe, gold woven in her hair, and carrying a golden quiver for her bows. Aeneas goes on ahead, and Dido spots him among the busy crowd of hunters, his beauty second only to that of the god Apollo.

The hunt travels through the valleys and forests, bands of Carthaginians and Trojans side by side. As they move, the skies begin to darken. What starts as a light drizzle quickly becomes wild rain and hail, scattering the hunting parties for cover wherever each person can find it across the fields and about the countryside. Dido and her Trojan leader find themselves sheltering alone in a cave. Juno nods her approval and lightning burns through the heavens. Their union there seals their fates. Dido no longer considers this a secret love affair; she feels they are now married as a couple. With her intensifying love, death creeps ever closer.

RUMOUR SPREADS

It doesn't take long for the goddess Rumour to fly through the cities of Libya. At speed, she carries salacious half-truths across the land from whispering lips to wagging tongues to inquisitive ears. Day and night the gossip seeps among the people of Dido's homeland: the Trojan who turned up one day, the queen who lowers herself to be with him, their shameless passion flaunted before everyone, how they spend all winter in unmarried lust, neglecting their duties to both the Carthaginian people and the Trojan refugees who seek their new home. Eventually the news reaches the ears of Jupiter, king of the gods. He summons the messenger god, Mercury, who flies in with his gold-winged boots.

'What is the meaning of this?' booms Jupiter across the heavens. 'Go tell that Aeneas to get his priorities straight. Doesn't he care that he has been given the greatest civilization to found on Italy's glorious land? Instead, does he want to cavort with the hostile Carthaginians? Will he deny his son Ascanius his future in leading Rome? What on earth does he think his plan is? Go and tell him this from me. This is Jupiter's message.'

AENEAS REALIZES HE MUST LEAVE

When Mercury appears before Aeneas, the Trojan is frozen in fear. The hairs on his arms stand on end and he is unable to utter a sound as he hears Jupiter's unyielding words. There is no mistaking the message from the king of the gods: Aeneas must leave Carthage immediately and continue on his mission to establish the city of Rome. The duty to his people must come before his personal desires. His mind races. What could he ever say to Dido, who is so intensely and powerfully in love? How could he even start that conversation? What words could possibly leave his lips to explain the inexplicable? Aeneas will need to work out the best way to approach his darling Dido. For now, he orders his men to ready the fleet. Jupiter has spoken and there cannot be any delay.

However, Rumour flies through the city once again, this time bringing to Dido's ears Aeneas' plans to leave. The queen flies through Carthage in a rage until she finds him. 'How dare you, Aeneas?' she screams. 'Doesn't our love mean anything to you? What about your promises to me? You'd rather set your ships into the wintery northern gales than stay here with me. Is it in fact me that you're fleeing from? Forget your far-flung destiny – if Troy were still standing, would you be heading there instead?'

Though Aeneas hears her cries, Jupiter's wrath keeps him steadfast on his mission, and with great pain, he pushes down the aching sorrow in his heart. 'Believe me, my queen, I was going to tell you I was leaving. I just didn't know how. This isn't my desire, but my duty. If Troy were still standing, I would be there and rule in it. But my people don't have a home like your Carthaginians do. Jupiter himself has warned me that I must keep going to Italy – there is my destiny.' Aeneas knows that nothing he can say will ease her dreadful agony, and heavy-hearted he returns to the fleet. His tears make no difference to her pain nor to his resolve.

A FIRE BURNS IN CARTHAGE

All across the shore, Trojan people pour out like columns of busy ants, heaving their possessions and supplies onto the many ships that line the sea. In the city, Dido is driven into a frenzy with intense hatred and love and fury and sorrow. She sees reminders of Aeneas everywhere: his clothes, his weapons, their marital bed, which now fill her with disgust. She will burn the lot. She instructs her sister Anna to have a huge fire built in the courtyard and she starts gathering Aeneas' possessions.

Anna worries about Dido's intentions as she watches her sister adorn the huge wooden pyre with wreaths and garlands, and have a couch set at the top of the rising structure. Dido lays one of Aeneas' thick robes onto the couch, and next to it his golden dagger and an image of the Trojan hero. Throughout the night, she readies the fire that will burn.

At first light, Aeneas orders the fleet to set sail. Dido's rage and passion drive her through the palace. In utter desperation she climbs uneasily up the towering pyre. She pulls herself to the top, where she is surrounded by Aeneas' familiar robe, his image and the dagger. She pulls the weapon from its sheath and, just as her maids rush into the courtyard, the queen falls down onto the blade. Screams fill the corridors and up to the ceilings of the sprawling palace.

Out to sea, Aeneas turns to look back to the city one last time. Such a soaring fire now glows from behind the palace walls, flickering orange across the dark sea. The flames of love that started in Dido's heart now burn on her own funeral pyre. Aeneas continues towards Rome.

Chapter 8
War

arfare is a prime backdrop to some of the most compelling and emotional struggles that humans can face. When confronting death and the survival of our homeland, we are driven to extreme actions. Existential threats to our life and livelihood push us to be our most passionate, our most brave and our most cunning.

Unsurprisingly then, many wars and conflicts provide the setting for myths around the world. The War of Troy is depicted in many examples of Greek and Roman literature, including Homer's *Iliad* and *Odyssey*, and Virgil's *Aeneid*; the Kurukshetra War features the mighty clash of cousins in the Ancient Indian epic *Mahabharata*; and many civilizations have told stories of warring between the gods to explain the existence of suffering, famine and floods down here on earth.

In much of our storytelling today, through the medium of film and television, a great battle scene provides wide-eyed fascination for any cinema audience. The same was true for the ancient storytellers of myth and legends. Extensive and detailed battle scenes are described in gruesome detail, with shining blades clashing, vast armies of men, horses and chariots colliding on the battlefield, and feats of extraordinary bravery and fearless foolishness.

Myths about war have given us the cunning Trojan Horse, but they have also created the environment for intense love and heart-breaking loss. You'll soon read about Aeneas desperately running through the dangerous streets of burning Troy in futile search of his wife Creusa. The same love and loss is sometimes told of comrades in war. The grief of Greek hero Achilles when his companion Patroclus is killed leads him to exact brutal and horrifying revenge on the prince of Troy.

War forces humankind to fiercely defend national pride. In doing so, it can be used in mythology to cement a national identity. A hero's struggle and ultimate triumph turns them into a role model of bravery, strength and behaviour. In one story in this chapter, from the *Bhagavad Gita* section of the *Mahabharata*, Arjuna travels to the battle line that has been drawn between two warring sides of the same family. As he sits between the armies on either side of him, he is forced to reflect on the futility of war. It sends him on a philosophical discourse with his companion Krishna on the nature of life, ethics and religion. The resulting conversation remains an important set of guidelines for the right way to live your life in the Hindu religion, even to this day. Similarly, the selflessness shown and tough decisions made by Aeneas as he departs the fallen city of Troy provide a protocol for the model citizen of the Roman Empire, for whom Aeneas' story was written.

THE TROJAN HORSE
ROMAN

The men waited silently inside the packed, wooden trunk of the horse. A single misstep would give them away. It would be certain death.

The legend of the Trojan Horse is so well known that it features in the literature of both the Ancient Greek and Roman civilizations, first appearing in works by Greek poet Homer, and later retold by Roman authors. The most extensive version of the myth comes to us through *The Aeneid*, the epic poem composed by Roman writer Virgil in the first century BC. As noted in the story of Aeneas and Dido (page 118), *The Aeneid* was commissioned by the Roman Empire's first emperor, Augustus Caesar, who was keen to inject some weight to his new-fangled dominion. There had been considerable unrest in the preceding decades, with civil wars, the dissolution of the Roman Republic and the assassination of Augustus' great uncle, Julius Caesar.

If Augustus Caesar was going to have any success with the formation of the Roman Empire, he would have to get citizens from across the Mediterranean behind his vision. He made huge improvements in infrastructure, social protection and undertook major construction in the city of Rome, as well as in the wider empire. He extended the borders of what was considered Roman in all directions, and as such, his rule is often associated with the Latin phrase *Pax Romana*, meaning 'Roman Peace'. It was a diplomatic way of describing the annexation of other people and lands into the Roman fold; it was peaceful only for those who complied, of course. But once you found your home was within the Roman Empire, it did come with the protection, perks and enforced *Pax* of being part of that federation.

Augustus was wise to realize that there is one thing that truly binds a nation together: its shared myths and legends. He commissioned already successful poet Virgil to compose the Roman Empire's very own mythical origin story. For centuries, the Romans had revered and romanticized the Greek epic poems of Homer, and both *The Iliad* and *The Odyssey* were classroom standards back then. (See more about Homer's *Odyssey* in Chapter 10: Epic Journeys.) As mentioned earlier, Virgil makes no apology for retelling the Greek myths from a Roman perspective, and borrows many themes and stories from the epic journey of Homer's *Odyssey*, and from the hard-fought wars of Homer's *Iliad*. In *The Aeneid*, our hero Aeneas makes his intrepid migration from the same War of Troy that features in Homer's works – albeit fighting for the other side, protecting Troy against Greeks like Odysseus. Once Troy has been sacked, Aeneas is told he must seek out a new homeland to form a great civilization. He visits weird and wonderful lands along the way, and eventually finds himself on the site upon which he will found the city of Rome. There, he wages war with the locals and the Roman civilization is born.

The whole epic gave Augustus Caesar the perfect scholarly weight for the formation of his Roman Empire. He wanted to convince Roman citizens across the Mediterranean that his wasn't just the latest political incarnation of the abandoned Republic, and all the war and unrest that came with that. Instead, the Empire was to be seen as the culmination of a centuries-long odyssey from the noble Greeks to the present day. Virgil does not in any way disguise the correlation that the reader is meant to make between the hero Aeneas and Augustus Caesar himself, both founding great civilizations.

Virgil's only challenge in rewriting Rome's origin story for his sponsor's political aims was that Rome already had a very famous genesis myth. That's the story of Romulus and Remus, the twin brothers who were abandoned by the River Tiber and found themselves being mothered by a wolf. The city is even named after one of those brothers. *The Aeneid* deftly intertwines the conflicting myths, claiming that Romulus and Remus are direct descendants of Aeneas. While he's at it, Virgil also draws an unbroken family line from Augustus Caesar up to Romulus, and all the way to the goddess Venus. What could bring greater credibility to the new Roman Empire?

Augustus knew the power of stories to unite people. A shared history – even if it is mythological – connects a society to its ancient roots. The strategy seems to have worked for him: he ruled until his natural death aged seventy-five, and even had the month of August named in his honour. The author Virgil, however, was less pleased with his *magnum opus*. On his deathbed, he instructed his friends to burn the manuscript, which remains unfinished. Luckily for Augustus' aims and for our own reading pleasure, Virgil's friends ignored the poet's dying wishes.

On page 120, we heard how Aeneas' brave stories wooed Queen Dido into falling in love with the hero. This following story about how the city of Troy came to be overthrown is a translation of one of those courageous tales.

AENEAS TELLS HIS STORY

The Greeks' attack on Troy is not going to plan. They are broken by war and close to defeat. They set their sights on one final attempt to sack the great city. With the help of the goddess Minerva, they build a towering horse from the wood of giant fir and maple trees. Its dark sides hide what lies inside: the strongest of the Greek soldiers are stowed in its belly. The rest of the army retreats to an offshore island, where they conceal themselves on its waterfront. There they watch and wait.

The massive horse is heaved to the grand gates of the walled city. The rumour spreads of a divine offering from the Greeks so that they might get safely home after so many years at war.

The Trojans rejoice at what seems to be the end of their sorrow and hardship. They wander out of the city walls, exploring the abandoned Greek camps, the deserted ships and the quiet shoreline. But what should they make of this gigantic offering that looms at the gates? Many want to haul it into the city. If this is an offering to the gods, it must be honoured. Troy can bear no more celestial wrath.

Others disagree. 'Pierce its sides!' they cry. 'Let's hurl it into the sea!'

One dubious citizen, Laocoön, cannot believe what his comrades are contemplating. 'Are you mad?' this priest of Neptune calls out. 'You really think the Greeks have just upped and left like that? Is that who you think the cunning Odysseus really is? Do not put your faith in this horse.'

Here, Laocoön utters a line for the ages: *timeo Danaos et dona ferentis* – 'Whatever this thing is, I fear Greeks – even when they bring gifts.'

With that, he hurls his sturdy spear solidly at the horse's vast flank. It pierces the wall with a distinctly hollow reverberation, followed by a man's sudden groan of death from within. A groan that should have given the Greeks away, had not at that very moment a noise from the crowd stifled the sound.

SINON CONVINCES THE TROJANS

A young Greek boy is being pushed through the throng with great commotion from the horde of people around him. His hands are tied. Is this all that remains of the cruel enemy army?

The frightened youth is presented to the taunts and gazes of the crowd, and speaks to King Priam of Troy. He tells how not all Greeks are the same, and that he should not be judged along with the other attackers.

'Odysseus and the other Greeks hated me,' the young Sinon begins. 'With so much defeat, they were desperate. The god Apollo told them that only a human sacrifice from within our ranks would help us to win this hopeless war.'

He tells the crowd, now with their weapons held down,

how his sacrifice was being prepared. Garlands adorned his head and food offerings were readied. Only by breaking free his tied hands was he able to escape death. Hiding in a dark and cold marsh, he concealed himself in the reeds until the Greeks had fled.

Feeling utter compassion for this poor boy at his story, King Priam tells him to renounce those wicked Greeks and welcomes him as an honorary citizen of Troy. Sinon has gained the trust of his former enemies, precisely as planned. Now for the real purpose of his placement in the opposition's city.

'From the start of this war a decade ago,' Sinon continues, 'the Greeks have relied on the goddess Minerva for all their victories. But their strength was shattered, they retreated, and the goddess distanced her affection.

'If Trojan hands should disrespect this offering to the almighty goddess, the gods will rain down utter destruction on your great city. But if you heave this holiest gift into the city walls, the destruction will fall on the Greeks instead. They will be entirely overthrown by Asian armies – the gods will see to it.'

A TERRIBLE OMEN

The Trojan people are already captivated by Sinon's tale and moved by his forced tears. In that moment, if they need any further convincing, comes a terrible omen. Laocoön, the priest of Neptune, is sacrificing a bull to the god of the seas, when from across the water come two mighty, coiled and twisting serpents.

They swim sinuously side by side towards the shore, casting a great wake behind them. As they approach the beach, they rise high above the crashing waves with their blood-red crests. Their terrible eyes are ablaze with fire and blood, and the panicking crowds scatter in terror as the serpents quickly cover ground and rush over to Laocoön's two sons. They lift the small children into the air, twisting and crushing, sinking fangs into their now lifeless bodies.

Laocoön charges the snakes in a hopeless attempt to save his boys. The serpents' scaly forms bend and fold high above the man, they encircle his waist and loop twice around his neck, dripping with black venom and blood. He lets out a horrendous cry to the heavens, matched only by the wails of the sacrificial bull, now running in a frenzy and shaking the axe from its gushing neck.

This is an indisputable message from the gods. Laocoön doubted the gift to Minerva and has paid the ghastly price. The mighty, wooden horse is dragged through the gates of Troy and into the city's heart. The Trojan people, unaware that this is their final day alive, hang decorations throughout the city and celebrate well.

The darkness of night falls, and the Trojans sleep. They can finally rest after so long under siege. They do not hear the Greeks silently sailing towards their shore from the island. They do not hear Sinon creeping through the streets towards the hollow offering to Minerva. They do not hear the Greek soldiers – cunning Odysseus himself in their company – emerge into the fresh air and slit the throats of the night watchmen.

TROY IS NO MORE

The city gates are opened from within, and the Greek army is welcomed in by its own men after so many years of war. Raging fire and clashing swords crash down on the people of Troy. Aeneas dreams that he is visited by the Trojan prince Hector, whose death is one of the most gruesome episodes in Homer's ancient poems.

'Get out now,' the apparition tells Aeneas in his dream. 'The city burns and the walls are breached. Troy itself trusts you now with the fate of its people. Go and seek that great city, which you will found after a long journey over the seas.'

Aeneas is conflicted by his duty to protect the city, and his obligation to seek out the new home for his people. He makes his way through the burning Troy, gathering comrades where he can. The homes of his friends and community are ablaze, and every instinct tells him to stay, to fight, to die in defending his homeland. Their weapons are worthless against such annihilation, but he and his men are raging like a ravenous pack of wolves, blind to the futility of the fight.

The Greeks pour through the streets in their thousands. Priam's palace – and then the elderly king himself – fall, and Aeneas finally realizes that Troy is no more. There is nothing left to fight for and he must go to rescue his own family.

Aeneas retreats from the combat to find his father Anchises, wife Creusa and son Ascanius. At his father's home, the ageing man is refusing to budge.

'You will be massacred, in the same way I have seen

King Priam slaughtered,' Aeneas protests. It is only when suddenly a harmless flame burns above little Ascanius' head, without hurting the boy, that Anchises changes his mind. The gods are on their side.

Aeneas' focus shifts from suicide to survival, and he lifts the old man onto his shoulders as they head through the blazing city. His wife Creusa must follow behind, and he agrees to meet the household and servants at an ancient cypress tree outside of the city. But the journey is not an easy one, and only when he reaches the meeting point does he see that his darling Creusa is no longer with him.

How did he lose her? Did she fall? Did she need to rest? Never again will his eyes see his beloved wife.

TROJANS IN EXILE

Aeneas leaves his father, son and servants, and frantically retraces his steps along the city walls and through the dangerous streets. Of all the destruction, bloodshed and inhumane horror that he has witnessed, this is the cruellest blow. Other than the raging fires around him, the city is silent – a dread fills his body with every noiseless corner he rounds back towards his home.

The Greeks, it seems, have made it here too. Aeneas fills the sky with his painful cries of misery – with no care as to whom, other than his wife, may hear them.

And suddenly, Creusa stands before him.

The hairs across his body stand on end. This is an apparition of his wife.

'Don't lose your head, darling,' his dead wife speaks to him. 'This is clearly the will of the gods. You have an important journey ahead of you, and you can't take me with you.'

She tells him of a far-distant land where the River Tiber flows, where he will found a great city and civilization. There's so much he wants to say to her, one last time, but she fades away before his eyes. Aeneas reaches out three times to touch her, and three times his hands clasp nothing but the cold night air. She is gone.

Aeneas returns to the cypress tree and, to his surprise, a crowd has built. From all over Troy, those that remain have come together. Mothers, men and children, all ready for the Trojan hero to lead them to a new home in a far-away land.

Aeneas lifts his father onto his shoulders once more and, as dawn begins to light the sky, he leads the exiles towards the mountains.

THE *BHAGAVAD GITA*
INDIAN

The *Bhagavad Gita* is an Ancient Indian poem, composed in Sanskrit during the period from 400 BC up until AD 400. It is one section of the epic poem *Mahabharata*, which tells of the terrible Kurukshetra War between the Pandava princes and their cousins, the Kaurava. The text is a fundamental guide for the Hindu religion to this day, telling of events that may have taken place up to one thousand years before they were committed to writing, and which were passed down orally from one generation to the next in the meantime. Spreading in that way through time and geography, there are several versions and revisions of this legend, and the exact composition of the text remains disputed.

The full *Mahabharata* is made up of eighteen *parvas* or books, and is attributed to the author Vyasa, who even appears in the narrative itself. It is the longest ancient epic poem in the world, comprising some 1.8 million words. It is ten times the length of both Homer's *Odyssey* and *Iliad* combined, and if you imagine stacking up forty-five copies of this book, you'll have a sense of the scale of the work.

The *Bhagavad Gita* falls in the sixth *parva*. The Pandava prince Arjuna is preparing for the great battle ahead, and starts to wonder what benefit there can be from all the death and violence that the Kurukshetra War will bring. He is accompanied by his charioteer Krishna, whose true divinity as an incarnation of Vishnu is gradually revealed. Arjuna asks his friend and guide questions about the rationale for war and Krishna answers. The dialogue between them covers many verses and extends far beyond war, with Krishna's answers providing a philosophical perspective on many aspects of how we should live our lives. He reveals the cyclical birth and rebirth of reincarnation, starts to reveal his own eternal presence in all living things, and advises on a life of non-violence. Krishna enlightens Arjuna on the impermanence of the human body and he encourages us to focus instead on the eternal Self – that soul that lives in many incarnations across time.

The detailed discourse on life, existence, ethics,

cosmology and more means that the *Mahabharata* – and particularly the *Bhagavad Gita* section – remains an important text for the Hindu religion, informing its lessons and traditions.

THE BATTLE LINES ARE DRAWN

The armies start to gather on opposite sides of the great battlefield. Many of the Kaurava fighters under King Dhritarashtra begin to look uneasily at the soldier beside them as the Pandava formations continue to swell. Arjuna is easy to spot in his chariot, and many equally accomplished warriors make up the substantial throng. They recognize many of the skilled archers now facing directly at them from a distance: these men nocking their arrows were once their comrades.

The Kaurava have many experienced heroes on their side too: Bhishma, Sanjaya and countless others, each ready and willing to die for the good of the many. Bhishma sees the unease of his army, so brings his giant conch shell to his lips. As he fills it with his breath, the conch's signal rises and vibrates until it roars like a lion. Within moments, thousands of conches, drums, trumpets and horns clamour forth a wall of sound.

On the other side, Arjuna is struck by the cacophony. He and Krishna raise their own conch shells in response, as do Bhima, King Dharmaraja, Nakalu and Sahadeo.

And so do the Maharaja of Benares, the great archer, and Shikhandi, the fearsome warrior. The reverberations violently shake the earth, boom across the heavens, and are felt in the heart of every Kaurava soldier.

ARJUNA'S ANGUISH

Looking across at the opposing army, lined up in formation and ready to fight, Arjuna's resolve falters. He speaks to his guide and charioteer: 'Krishna, I ask you: please let's take my chariot to the very battle line between the two armies. I need to see those men who must fight on my side, and I want to look into the eyes of those men who are willing to die for King Dhritarashtra.'

Krishna does as he is asked and draws up the chariot directly between the two clans. Arjuna slowly scans the fighters to his left and right, and his heart breaks. He sees fathers, grandfathers, uncles, sons, grandsons, teachers, friends and fathers-in-law lined up in regiments on both sides.

'Oh, Krishna!' Arjuna cries. He stumbles in the chariot and drops his arms by his side. The hairs stand up on his neck and his hands visibly tremble. 'I can barely stand up,' he continues. 'My throat is dry and I feel like I'm on fire. My mind is all over the place. What good can come from massacring my own people on this battlefield? I don't crave the victory, I don't need the crown, I get no joy from this. What good is a kingdom or happiness to me, when the people I want those things for sacrifice their own lives in my pursuit of it?

'Standing in lines before me, I see teachers, fathers, grandfathers, sons and grandsons, uncles, fathers-in-law, brothers-in-law – everyone's related to someone here! I could not kill any of them, even for three worlds, let alone for this one desperate world.'

KRISHNA AND ARJUNA'S DISCOURSE BEGINS

'Surely we're better than this,' Arjuna's torment continues. 'Greed is blinding these men to kill their own family, but we have our eyes open. Shouldn't we turn our backs on destroying our home? If we butcher our own people, we're butchering generations of ancient tradition that has been passed down through our bloodline.'

Arjuna starts to see it all clearly now. 'If we massacre our own traditions, what are we left with? No religion, no purity, no morals. Promiscuity and adultery may as well take over. No funeral rituals to ensure our ancestors' souls are cared for. A civilization that loses its traditions is lost forever.

'And here we stand, ready to kill our fellow citizens – for the temporary joy of a kingdom. Surely I'd be far better off if King Dhritarashtra's army got me now, unarmed and putting up no fight!'

There in his chariot, in the very midst of the two armies poised to launch at each other, Arjuna sinks into his seat. The lethal bow in his hand drops to the floor. He and Krishna retreat slowly back to the ranks of their own side, and Arjuna's anguish turns into curiosity and searching as he seeks Krishna's counsel on life's most important questions. Facing war, death and destruction of one family against its own cousins, Arjuna is driven to contemplate the war raging within each person: between our duty and our destiny.

Chapter 9
Monsters and Spirits

antastical monsters and magical beasts are perhaps the hallmark of mythological folklore the world over. These are legends after all, rather than real-life stories, and so the storytellers can let their imaginations run wild with all the creatures that a hero might encounter on their fictitious journey. From monkey kings, to snake-haired ogres, to three-headed dogs, there is no limit to what an audience might happen upon as they listen to and retell the legends of their ancestors.

Fantasy and inventiveness make for great stories. But more than that, monsters can provide an important role for the audience: in seeing some of the grotesque and lawless beasts that are out there beyond our own known world, we are forced to consider who we are. The sense of otherness in these creatures galvanizes what it means *not* to be other. In this way, authors and storytellers invite the audience to cement their own identity as a society.

Mythology has been used by every civilization on the planet to explain the inexplicable. A narrative, unpredictable spirits and beasts, and a triumphant hero made it easier for our ancestors to make sense of struggles such as illness, death, drought and floods. Where knowledge was lacking, erratic monsters and spirits – and the heroes to conquer them – stepped in to provide an account that was as comprehensible as it was entertaining.

So, look beyond the serpentine hair of Medusa, and you'll find a story of what it means to be Greek, what it means to be brave, and how trust in the gods can help any Greek citizen overcome the biggest challenges.

MEDUSA
GREEK AND ROMAN

The snake-haired Medusa is a well-known image of Ancient Greece. With terrible serpents entwining around her head, ferocious tusks and wild eyes that would turn you to stone with one misjudged glimpse, it's hard to imagine that her beauty was once the envy of the gods. In fact, it was Medusa's former hair that was most admired about her, and that enticed the god of the seas, Poseidon, to violate her in a temple of Athena. That goddess was so affronted by the deed that she sought to punish Medusa's beauty – rather than Poseidon's violation – and turned her into the hideous Gorgon we've come to know. Some of the detail of Medusa's previous beauty is a Roman addition to the Greek myth. In Ancient Greece, she was one of a family of hideous monsters that simply needed killing, and the Greek hero to do just that was Perseus.

The practice of Romans taking on Greek legends and elaborating them with their own details and versions is precisely what folklore is all about. In fact, early Greek texts make no mention of snakes in her hair at all. All mythologies of the world have survived because of the retelling of their legends from one generation to the next. Reading the tales again in this book is one link in an unceasing chain of storytellers that stretches back to the beginning of humanity, and has not stopped yet. The legend of Medusa is first documented in Homer's Greek *Iliad* in around 700 BC, with further details explained by Apollodorus and others in the first century BC. The Romans then take up the baton, among them Ovid in his AD 8 poem *Metamorphoses*, and my retelling here is made from a combination of the Greek and Roman versions.

But the chain does not stop there. In the story of Medusa, the hero Perseus must first meet the three haggard old sisters of Medusa known as the Graeae. It is possible that the three witches at the start of Shakespeare's *Macbeth* (those of the famous line 'Double, double, toil and trouble'), written around AD 1600, are characters influenced by these three Graeae sisters. Shakespeare borrows heavily from classical mythology, and lifts plots – and in fact entire passages – from Ovid's *Metamorphoses* for several of his plays, including *Romeo and Juliet*, *A Midsummer Night's Dream* and *The Tempest*.

Once Shakespeare had cemented it, the trope of three wicked witches became etched in the cultural psyche. They can be seen in various movies, for example: *The Witches of Eastwick* (1987), *Hocus Pocus* (1993 – and its 2022 sequel, of course) and *Stardust* (2007), to name a few. It is another reminder that the latest films, the most recent novels and the ancient poems of the Romans alike are all part of a breadcrumb trail of legends that has been added to by countless generations, each one borrowing from and embellishing on the generation before it.

A BAD OMEN

King Acrisius of Argos seems not to be able to sire a male heir to his throne. Desperate, he seeks out advice from the soothsaying Oracle at Delphi. The entranced priestess spits forth a terrible omen for Acrisius: it is not a son he should be concerned about, but a male grandson, who will grow up to kill the king. Terrified for his life, Acrisius rushes home to Argos and immediately sets about imprisoning his daughter Danaë in an underground bronze chamber, with just one opening to the sky.

While imprisoned here, Danaë incredibly becomes pregnant. The king of Mount Olympus, Zeus himself, is so taken by the beautiful girl that he disguises himself as a golden rain that showers down onto her and gives her a son, Perseus. When Acrisius discovers the child, he locks both Perseus and Danaë in a chest and has it cast out to sea. Despite the odds stacked against them, mother and son wash safely ashore on the island of Seriphus, where the boy is raised by King Dictys.

AN IMPOSSIBLE TASK

The king's brother Polydectes gradually falls in love with Danaë, and as Perseus grows into a young man, Polydectes feels it's time to get rid of him. Polydectes throws a huge banquet in honour of a noble wedding, and demands that all his friends provide horses as a gift – knowing full well that Perseus has no such thing to offer. Eager to please, Perseus declares that he has no horse, but that he will gladly bring any gift that Polydectes can name. The scheming brother sees his opportunity: 'Bring me the head of Medusa. One look on her gruesome face will turn any man to stone. But you did ask me to name my gift.'

Daunted by the impossible task but intent on victory, Perseus prays to Hermes and Athena for guidance on how to tackle such a monster. The gods advise him to seek out the nymphs of Hesperides, who will be able to guide him on how to defeat the hideous and deadly Medusa. Perseus travels to far-away lands until he finds the three Graeae sisters, Medusa's own siblings who have been grey and old since birth. The three wicked witches have only one eye and one tooth that they pass between them to see and to speak. At first, they are no help to Perseus, and he realizes he must grab their attention another way. Just as one of the beastly trio passes the bulging eye from her hand to her sister's, Perseus snatches it away. Blinded and tricked, the Graeae cry out in ferocious anger.

'Show me the way to the Hesperides nymphs!' Perseus calls out. 'Then you may see again.'

PERSEUS DEFEATS MEDUSA

The Graeae give in to the hero's demands, and he continues his journey to the furthest lands in the west and to the Hesperides. There, the nymphs furnish him with the weapons he will need: winged sandals from the messenger god Hermes, a mighty diamond sword from Zeus, a pouch in which to carry the decapitated head of Medusa – to avoid her stare turning him to stone even in her death – and the invisibility helmet from Hades of the Underworld. With these items, Perseus hides himself from view and flies across the ocean to find his foe.

Perseus finds Medusa asleep in a cave, surrounded by other Gorgons. Guided by the gods, he dare not look directly at the monster, but glances instead at the reflection of her in the shimmering bronze shield strapped to one arm. The breath leaves his body and the hairs on his neck stand on end. He steadies his shield and looks again. Around her head are entwined black dragon scales and sinuous serpentine hair, great boars tusks jut out from her hideous mouth, she rests on solid bronze hands and her mighty, golden wings are folded behind her.

Athena is looking down on the hero. She strengthens his hand and guides him towards the odious Medusa while he looks only at the reflected image. He raises the magnificent diamond sword and with all his strength cuts off her deadly head. In that moment of death, blood spews forth from her neck, and out with it rush her final offspring: the winged horse Pegasus and his warrior brother Chrysaor. The Gorgons around her awake with screeches that reverberate about the cave and shake the ground. In a moment, Perseus grabs the writhing, blood-soaked head and stashes it in his pouch. He puts on the invisibility helmet once more to make his escape.

ATLAS IS PUNISHED

As Perseus flies across the deserts of Libya, thick blood spills from the sinewy head he carries. As each heavy blotch hits the land below, it turns into countless snakes that now infest the land. Flying as high as the clouds and brushing the stars with his beating wings, Perseus is driven across the world by winds that blow in all directions, far to the east then far to the west. Three times he sees the frozen north and three times he sees the Cancer constellation.

Finally he passes near to the Hesperides and to the kingdom of the giant Atlas – there he will surely find shelter. 'I am Perseus, son of Zeus,' the weary hero tells his host. 'I ask for hospitality and rest on my long journey home.'

Atlas' eyes widen. This is surely the terrible prophecy that he was once told: that one day a son of Zeus will come to steal away the golden apples that he has guarded by a dragon in a walled garden. Terrified that the omen has come to pass, Atlas turns Perseus away. 'Get away from my garden!' the gargantuan king cries as he shoves Perseus with his mighty weight.

Knowing he cannot match Atlas' strength, Perseus fights back only with calm words: 'Very well. If you show me so little kindness, accept this gift from me.' With that, he turns his own head and lifts hideous Medusa's from his pouch. In an instant, Atlas is turned into a towering stone mountain. His hair and beard become the trees on top of the peak that still bears his name. His bones petrify into gigantic rocks and the mountain is lifted up to the very stars.

PERSEUS RETURNS HOME

Perseus eventually makes his way home, not just to the island of Seriphus, but to his rightful home of Argos. King Acrisius, who cast Perseus out to sea all those years ago, is terrified that the Oracle's prophecy will come to pass – that he will be killed by his own grandson – and the king flees to the other side of Greece to the land of the Palasgians. But you cannot run from your fate. The king of the Palasgians throws a celebratory feast and games in honour of his late father, and Perseus, now known as a divine hero and warrior, is invited to compete in the pentathlon. In one game, he hurls a heavy, metal ring to reach its target – which, in a way, it does. It strikes Acrisius and the king dies instantly.

For her guidance in his seemingly impossible task, Perseus offers the head of Medusa to the goddess Athena, who immortalizes the serpentine monster in her shield. Many of the depictions of Athena in art and sculpture show her bearing the shape of Medusa's head in her armour.

GRENDEL

ANGLO-SAXON

Grendel is a fearsome monster that terrorizes the halls of a great Danish king, devouring his strongest warriors as they sleep. He is one of the central beasts of the Old English epic poem *Beowulf*, which tells of a hero by that name who battles mythical monsters and legendary dragons. Composed in England by an unknown author in about AD 1000, the poem's only surviving manuscript was written on worm-eaten and fire-damaged parchment, seemingly by two different scribes. The handwriting noticeably changes mid-sentence about two-thirds of the way through the more than three thousand lines of poetry, and the language markedly shifts to more archaic forms of Old English.

Beowulf chiefly focuses on three battles that Beowulf must fight. The first is against the monster Grendel, to defend King Hrothgar's people. The second is against Grendel's mother, who seeks revenge for her son's death. And the third is against a ferocious dragon, which has been destroying villages. Beowulf is victorious in all three fights, but ultimately dies from the injuries he sustains in the final battle.

The epic poem is England's answer to the foundational literary works enjoyed by the Greeks in Homer's *Iliad* or by the Romans in Virgil's *Aeneid*. It tells of a distant time before the Germanic tribes settled in England, mixing Norse, Christian and other mythologies in its verses. This blending of influences reflects the complex cultural and religious merging that was taking place as different groups collided on English soil.

The influence of *Beowulf* is so far-reaching in our storytelling that the idea of the hero slaying a dragon seems almost mundane to our modern ears. J.R.R. Tolkien's *The Lord of the Rings* makes no attempt to hide its strong connection with *Beowulf.* Tolkien saw the poem as a cornerstone of English literary tradition and he published academic works about it, before writing his own version of an epic poem based on a mythical England. The 'Middle-earth' in which his stories take place is borrowed from the Norse name also given to the human realm in *Beowulf.*

In this part of the Old English poem, we hear how Beowulf must fight and ultimately conquer the terrible beast, Grendel.

ONCE UPON A TIME IN A FAR-AWAY LAND

Heralding from a long line of noble and well-admired warriors, King Hrothgar of the spear-armoured Danes is glorious in war and is dutifully followed by his people. He resolves that he will raise a grand feasting hall to house his loyal soldiers, and gathers workers from tribes far and wide to build the structure. The name of Heorot, the largest construction ever seen, grows famous across Middle-earth. And King Hrothgar does not hold back on his promise to feast and celebrate there: the sound of harps and songs rises to the heavens from every banquet. Bards sing of God and of the legends of man and the earth.

The joy and revelry touches everybody, except for one. The grim monster Grendel grows angrier and more furious with each festive song. He is part of the unspeakable offspring of ogres, elves, evil spirits and giants fathered by Cain, the man who, in the book of Genesis, murders his own brother Abel. Since then, they have been exiled here by God himself to be hidden from humankind for the terrible crime.

GRENDEL VISITS

One night, after another beer-fuelled banquet, the unholy creature wanders up to the high hall and sees all the noblemen fast asleep and oblivious to the outside world. Grim and greedy, the gruesome Grendel snatches up thirty warriors from their slumber, and strolls back homewards for a banquet of his own. Only when dawn lights up the hall do King Hrothgar and his men see what has happened while they slept. The king cries out in sorrow at losing so many loyal men, and his anguish is only made worse when he realizes how they met their end.

The following night, ruthless Grendel returns. Violence and viciousness don't bother him at all, and he grabs at a few more of this fine community of warriors. Again and again, the beast visits and no man can hide from his grasp. For twelve terrible winters, the relentless attacks continue, until almost no man is left standing in that mighty hall any longer. News of the death shadow that lurks around the corners of once-great Heorot spreads far across Middle-earth, until it reaches the Geat clan across the sea and one hero in particular: Beowulf.

BEOWULF ARRIVES IN HEOROT

Not every one of Hrothgar's noblemen is pleased to see the young hero come to save them from across the water. Unferth, a seasoned fighter, can't believe that this youth thinks he can overcome such a beast as Grendel – stealing the glory for himself.

'I've heard about you, Beowulf,' Unferth tells the visitor. 'I've heard plenty of stories about your seafaring bravado, but also about how some of your glories aren't all they seem to be. You think you can simply hide in the night and wait for Grendel. I'll tell you how this fight will end.'

'Don't you doubt me, Unferth,' Beowulf counters, 'drunk on beer as you are. Many men and monsters have died by my sword. If you were as fierce in battle as you'd like to portray, dreadful Grendel would never have been able to commit such massacre again and again, and bring humiliation to the name of Heorot. He doesn't even need to fight. You're famous as the spear-armoured Danes, and yet Grendel faces no combat as he delights his lust and picks your men off one by one. Let him meet the strength and courage of the Geats. Another dawn will shine over the sons of Heorot.'

For the first time in many years, the melody of celebration and laughter fills the hall. The victory chants of champions lift to the ceiling. Adorned in gold, Queen Wealhtheow of Heorot offers beer to all the men one by one, young and old, until eventually she reaches Beowulf. He looks at her resolutely and quietly reassures her: 'When I set sail from Geatland with my men, I resolved that I would help your people or that I would die trying.'

BEOWULF AWAITS GRENDEL

Night falls and Hrothgar eventually seeks rest. Ever since dusk, he's known that Grendel is planning his next attack on the high hall. Others bid their farewell and offer words of courage, as the king speaks to the young hero: 'Since the day I could lift up my spear and shield, I have never entrusted the fate of my people and my grand hall to any man. And now I trust you. Keep your focus on victory, show great courage, be vigilant and hold this greatest of houses safely in your hands. You will never want for anything if you come out of this brave mission with your life.'

The hall empties and Beowulf bravely entrusts his mission to the mercy of God. He sets aside his iron armour, removes the helmet from his head, and gives his ornate sword to one of his men to guard. As he settles in his own sleeping spot, the Geat prince makes a promise: 'I am no worse in the art of fighting than Grendel himself. We are equally matched, and so I will not slay him with my sword, even though I could. If this beast seeks out a fight without weapons, that's what I will give him – and God will choose the right victor.' Beowulf sinks down to rest, surrounded by his men, each of them wondering whether they will see their home again after this night.

GRENDEL ENTERS THE HALL

From the dark moorlands comes a noise. Vile Grendel, heavy with the wrath of God, has human flesh in his sights as he storms towards the golden hall. Beowulf is alert as the large doors fly open, the iron bolts cast aside as Grendel pushes through. The hideous creature strides aggressively across the hall, and Beowulf can see fire flashing in his eyes as they wildly scan the room full of delicious prey.

With a swift move, the monster grabs a sleeping warrior. Beowulf looks in horror as Grendel tears the man from limb to limb, biting through to the bones, sucking out the blood and devouring his comrade piece by piece until nothing remains. Grendel lunges forward towards another sleeping warrior – a plumper one this time – and as his arm reaches out, now Beowulf's hand clamps down on the brute's hand. Never in all of Middle-earth has the beast felt such a grip as this. His heart races and he struggles to break free, desperate to get back to his hellish home.

Beowulf thinks back to the bold promises he made that evening, and leaps up to tighten his grip on Grendel, who grapples to heave his arm back. Each time the creature is able to make a move towards the great doors, the hero is around him and wrestles tighter still. The Danes awake and a din rumbles around the hall as they watch the two fighters clash and tumble across the mighty room.

Vast benches adorned with gold are sent flying and are smashed to pieces – a wonder that the great hall itself is not destroyed by the battling enemies. Beowulf's men look on in terror as the beast's wailing cries of defeat reverberate around the walls.

GRENDEL IS KILLED

Beowulf has no intention of letting Grendel get out alive. His men now raise their ancient swords and charge the howling beast from all sides, and yet as they lunge forward, each of their iron blades is unable to pierce his thick hide. This mystic spell means his miserable death will not come swiftly. Beowulf tightens his grip on the ogre's arm, until a gaping wound in his shoulder widens, sinews spring asunder, and monstrous muscles burst out.

Mortally wounded, Grendel stumbles out of the shaken hall and into the darkness to find his final resting place. The Danes delight at this triumph of the brave and bold wandering hero over the beast that has tormented them for so long. Proof of the final victory is lying in the middle of the hall: Grendel's arm and shoulder beneath its vaulted ceiling.

Chapter 10
Epic Journeys

f all the variations of myth that have been passed down through generations of storytellers, those that tell of epic journeys are perhaps the most captivating. From Australia's First Nations to the Middle East to the Greeks and Romans, people have been weaving elaborate stories of life-threatening expeditions for millennia.

Though some of these examples have borrowed from each other across the boundaries of time and geography, many of the legends were crafted completely independently of one another. And yet, they often share many of the same features.

In 1949, American academic Joseph Campbell categorized the hero's journey into three distinct stages: the Departure, in which the hero is called to his mission; the Initiation, during which he must endure multiple challenges and tests; and finally the Return, in which he journeys home as a new man.

During the Departure stage, our hero – typically a young man – is going about his life nicely. At some point, an existential threat calls him, somewhat unwillingly, to make an extraordinary quest. Following some initial resistance to step into the shoes of a hero, our protagonist meets a mentor, deity or guide, who helps him to see the importance of the journey he must embark upon.

The second stage is usually the fun part. The far wandering of his Initiation stage gives licence to poets, writers and storytellers across the ages to let their imagination conjure up all sorts of wonderful and fantastical beasts, monsters and gods for the hero to encounter. Medieval nautical maps used to state *Here Be Dragons* for any unchartered areas of the world – and ancient storytellers were no different in their myths. Unknown, far-away lands were assumed to be chock-full of extraordinary alien creatures. Some are dreadful and out for our hero's blood, while others will guide and help him along his treacherous journey.

Finally, he makes his way home in the Return stage of the journey, with a new sense of identity. Only by witnessing such strange and magical worlds over the edge of the map does the hero truly understand who he is and what he holds valuable.

The hero's epic journey is a tradition that has continued in storytelling to the modern day. The same overall plot can be seen in *The Lord of the Rings*, *Star Wars*, and *Harry Potter*.

In this chapter, you will hear about three legendary journeys. First is the Mesopotamian tale of Gilgamesh and a very mighty flood, one of the oldest written pieces of literature in existence. Second, comes the Songlines of Australia's First Nations. The third journey tells of the Greek hero Odysseus deceiving the mighty, one-eyed Cyclops.

GILGAMESH AND THE GREAT FLOOD

MESOPOTAMIAN

There once was a storm so ferocious that even the gods trembled with fear and cowered like terrified dogs. The flood that followed the storm flattened the land and killed almost every person. However, a handful of fortunate people survived.

The legend is depicted in the *Epic of Gilgamesh* and was first told by the Sumerians as early as 2100 BC, later intricately engraved onto large stone tablets. The Sumerians are the first known civilization in Mesopotamia, an area whose name literally means 'between the rivers', as it was situated between the Euphrates and Tigris rivers in modern-day Iraq. Gilgamesh was the king of the city of Uruk. His adventures, misadventures, dealings with the gods and pursuit of meaning form one of the earliest pieces of literature in existence, transporting the legends directly from the mouths of the ancient Sumerians to our own imaginations four millennia later.

Of all the myths that were brought together to form the *Epic of Gilgamesh*, the recounting of the great flood is particularly interesting. It tells of Gilgamesh's search for meaning and immortality, following the death of his friend. What makes it a notable tale among all the others is its familiarity. Anyone who has read the story of Noah's Ark and *his* great flood, recounted in both the Bible and the Qur'an many hundreds of years later, will get a distinct sense of *déjà vu* when hearing about Gilgamesh's deluge.

THE DEATH OF A FRIEND

Gilgamesh's friend Endiku has died. Following a disagreement with the gods, it was decreed that one of the two men must meet their end. Endiku pulled the short straw, and now, pacing up and down and exchanging emotional and desperate words as his friend nears his final hours, Gilgamesh has had to watch from his companion's bedside as he declines into death. Gilgamesh is overcome with deep grief. Inconsolable, he calls on all the people of Uruk – and the very land itself – to share the unbearable sorrow for his friend.

'May the elders of the broad city of Uruk mourn you! May the men of the mountains and hills mourn you. May the very pasture lands cry out in mourning as if they were your mother. May the bear, the hyena, the panther, tiger, jackal, lion, wild bull, stag, ibex, all the creatures of the plains mourn you. May the holy river Ujala, along whose banks we used to stroll, mourn you!'

He can see that Endiku's body is lifeless, that his eyes don't move, and he can feel no heartbeat in his body. Gilgamesh cries out. He cuts his hair off in grief and tears the luxurious robes from his body in disgust. His riches are futile now. For six days and seven nights, Gilgamesh mourns Endiku. Heartbroken, he refuses to believe that his companion's life is over. It's not until he sees a maggot drop to the ground from his most loved friend's nose that he has no choice but to accept his parting and allow his burial.

A LONG JOURNEY

Feeling helpless and hopeless, Gilgamesh starts to consider his own mortality.

'I am going to die! Am I not just like Enkidu?' he calls out. 'This deep, deep sadness penetrates me to my very core. I don't want to die!'

Gilgamesh resolves that only one thing can assuage his desperation: an epic journey to visit a man called Utnapishtim, far away at the ends of the earth, who is rumoured to have mastered the tricky art of immortality. Gilgamesh would make the perilous expedition to discover the secret to dodging death. His journey sees him slaying lions, negotiating with scorpion-people, braving absolute pitch-dark lands, and traversing the ominously named Waters of Death to reach Utnapishtim. There, finally, Gilgamesh learns a tale so secret that even the gods were deceived by it.

UTNAPISHTIM'S TALE

Utnapishtim begins his story of how he gained immortality. In the city of Shuruppak – ancient even in Gilgamesh's days – lived both people and gods. The deities had agreed between them that they would send a great storm and flood to clear the city of its people. The king of the gods, Anu, made the decree, advised by Enlil, Ninurta and Annugi, but the godly prince Ea had other ideas. They were all sworn to secrecy and were not to tell the mortals, so instead Ea whispered the secrets into the reed-lined walls of Utnapishtim's home.

Through the walls, Utnapishtim heard the god's instructions: 'Tear down your house and build a boat!'

Unfazed by his speaking house, he listened as prince Ea's words continued: 'Abandon all your wealth and value living beings instead. Abandon all your possessions and keep people and animals alive instead. Get them all into the boat, which you must build.'

If questioned by his neighbours, Utnapishtim was to tell them that he had angered the god Enlil and therefore was unwelcome on his land. He was to report that he was moving away from Shuruppak and down the river to an area favoured by Ea, where he would be safe. In return, he was to tell them, Ea would shower down on them wheat, loaves of bread, meat and fish. Utnapishtim assembled all the workers he could to help him build the massive ark. Carpenters, weavers and even children were enrolled to get to work on the seven-storey construction. Each storey was divided into nine compartments, and he set about making the whole structure watertight with unimaginable quantities of pitch and bitumen, and with huge wooden plugs driven into the boat's towering hull.

He paid the workers in beer, wine and meat, and put on a party as debaucherous as a new year's festival. The boat was ready to launch. Two vast tracks were made from tree trunks to haul the massive vessel partway into the water, and Utnapishtim loaded the boat with everything he owned. Each of his friends, family and the craftsmen (and, one assumes, the crafts-children who also helped) were given one of the enviable seats onboard. All the creatures, beasts and land-working animals were loaded, and the ark was sealed.

Then, just as dawn began to glow, the storm came. The gods rose thick, black clouds over the horizon. The rain god Adad rumbled and shook inside them. Darkness covered the land. The twins of destruction, Shullat and Hanish, blew ferocious gales across the terrain. Nergal, the god of death, broke the ark away from its moorings, as Anunnaki lifted up his torches and set the land ablaze. Mountains were pounded by water and the Shuruppak homeland shattered like a clay pot.

The gods themselves were utterly terrified by what they saw. They retreated up to the heavens with King Anu. They cowered like dogs, they wailed out like a woman in childbirth, and they wept as they watched for seven days how the storm battered and fought the land. On the seventh day, calmness finally spread across Shuruppak once again. The storm had subsided and Utnapishtim opened a vent to take a deep breath of fresh air for the first time and to feel the daylight on his face. He saw all around that the earth had been flattened by the ferocious storm, and an eerie silence revealed to him that every person had been turned to clay. He fell to his knees and wept.

The ark had been swept up into the mountains and was now lodged firmly on Mount Nimush. Still, all that Utnapishtim could see around him was water. He sent a dove out to look for land, but it flew around and soon returned. Likewise, when he sent out a swallow, it flew off but soon returned. Only when he sent the third bird, a raven, did he notice that the waters were receding and the bird didn't return. This was the sign to him that he could start releasing all the animals back onto the land.

Utnapishtim burnt an incense offering to the gods from reeds, cedar and myrtle. As his offering blazed, a winding column of sweet smoke snaked up to the heavens, and the gods crowded round like flies on a sacrificed sheep. The god Enlil was furious to see that his plan hadn't worked and that some of the people of Shuruppak had survived. The prince Ea was immediately suspected.

With a bit of convincing, Ea's pleas to Enlil made him see how needlessly destructive his flood had been to humanity. He appealed to Enlil to bless Utnapishtim and his wife with immortality. With his arm twisted, Enlil stepped into the ark and, grasping Utnapishtim by the hand, brought both him and his wife to the gods. There they knelt as Enlil touched their foreheads and granted them everlasting life among the gods.

GILGAMESH RETURNS HOME
SADDER BUT WISER

Gilgamesh is gobsmacked by the tale of the flood. He will do anything to join Utnapishtim in immortality, but it seems to have been a very unique gift in an exceptional circumstance, rather than something he can simply request. As if to prove this, Utnapishtim sets a challenge to Gilgamesh: if he can stay awake for six days and seven nights like they had to during the storm, he will be granted immortality.

Barely has Utnapishtim uttered those words, when Gilgamesh instantly falls asleep. Utnapishtim's wife bakes a loaf of bread for each day that our hero is out for the count. It's not until seven loaves later that Gilgamesh's hosts shake him awake and send him on his way, seemingly with a new-found realization that his quest for immortality is over.

SONGLINES
ABORIGINAL AUSTRALIAN

The Songlines of Australia's First Nations offer a different perspective of the hero's journey. These physical pathways across the Australian continent are trading routes and directions to sacred sites, accompanied by songs that act as musical maps to guide the traveller's passage. More than myth, these routes are very real, and the hero of them is any member of each specific community who chooses to undertake the journey.

The stories of Aboriginal Australian peoples are inextricably linked to the land around them. Travelling and trading across the vast continent, they created music that sang of particular routes, recognizable animals and land formations. They were melodic and rhythmic memory banks that allowed the traveller to know where along the Songline they were by the features they had passed, where to find watering holes, where the boundaries between communities lay, and what animals and plants they would likely encounter on the way. The Songlines – physical paths and the songs that represent them – became part of the identities of the First Nations that sang each one. They speak of social laws of how to treat other nations, who to marry, and how to behave when visiting other communities.

The stories told in the Songlines can even transcend language. Certain rhythms and sound patterns in the music, the dances and in the playing of the *yidaki* (the didgeridoo) sometimes reference animals and landforms that make up the Songlines. In this way, regardless of which nation you came from and which language you spoke, you had the map of the route if you knew the song.

For nations whose history wasn't written down, and whose culture has been systematically suppressed, the only connection to their ancient ancestors lies in the stories and songs that are passed down. These narratives may be ten thousand years old or more, and only remain today because of an unbroken sequence of grandfathers, grandmothers and parents who have retold them for countless generations.

Many of the pathways that make up the Songlines were well-worn trails by the time colonizers invaded Australia in 1788. This made them ideal routes for the growing population of foreigners to start traversing the continent, and several of these ancient spiritual walkways have over time been turned into the network of roads and highways of Australia.

This story of the Seven Sisters is inspired by the Warlpiri people, whose land is in the Tanami Desert north-west of Alice Springs. As the narrative travels across the Australian terrain, versions of it are picked up by other peoples, and many variants of the legend exist. For more about the belief systems of First Nations Australians, see Chapter 1, under The Dreamtime.

THE SEVEN SISTERS

Soon after the sun sets and the last of her red dye has coloured the sky, seven shimmering stars rise up from the horizon. They are seven Napaljarri ancestors – sisters who are visible in the twilight and who stay close to the land as they move quickly across the sky. They seem to be running from something.

Not long after, their pursuer shows himself: Jukurra-jukurra, the Jakamarra ancestor, wants to take one of the sisters for his wife. He appears in the night at dusk as he tracks the sisters across the heavens, never letting them out of his sight.

Continually, they are pursued by the man, even though tradition says this Jakamarra man is the wrong skin name to marry these Napaljarri sisters. Continually, they must flee, and as they travel across the land to make their escape, they form hills, jutting rocks and watering holes to hide from Jukurra-jukurra.

They finally trick him by carving a deep watering hole into the rocks, which travels cavernously underground before emerging on the other side of a small hill. The quick-witted sisters dive into the watering hole and make their escape, while Jukurra-jukurra is too late to catch them after he finally emerges. The sisters launch themselves into the night sky where, every evening, the seven stars of the Pleiades constellation are still pursued by the brightly visible planet Venus at dusk.

THE ODYSSEY
GREEK

There once lived a man who was cunning, a good fighter and who commanded twelve large ships on their way home from a long war. But Poseidon, the god of the sea, had other intentions for Odysseus and his men. In the end, our hero would be the only man from the 600-strong crew to survive and make it home.

The Odyssey comprises about twelve thousand lines of poetry, composed in Greece sometime around 700 BC. Attributed to the poet Homer, it tells the legend of the hero Odysseus, as he makes his journey home from the War of Troy. It is the same bloody war that is described in the story of The Trojan Horse (page 129), which is told from the viewpoint of the other side. In fact, Odysseus is one of the Greek soldiers hiding inside the wooden horse that leads to Troy's defeat.

Odysseus has been at war for ten whole years, and doesn't quite expect his commute back to Ithaca to take another decade of challenges and adventure. While his wife Penelope sits at home, batting away would-be suitors for twenty years, Odysseus and his men accidentally take a wrong turn out of Troy and end up sailing the picturesque route across the Mediterranean to get home. Along the way, they encounter all manner of beastly beasts, benevolent gods, vengeful deities and everything in between.

Odysseus' son Telemachus has grown up in the meantime, and makes his own quest to find his father. The boy's name literally means 'far from the war', to epitomize how he has had to become the man of the household and watch his mother mourn the missing hero while war raged on in far-away Troy. After ten years of the most extraordinary exploits, Odysseus returns to the palace in Ithaca and slays all of the suitors encircling his wife, in gruesome scenes of vengeance.

One of the most extraordinary things about Homer's *Odyssey* is that it was composed before Greek writing was even invented. Think about that for a moment. Thousands and thousands of lines of poetry and intricate storytelling that could only be passed on, one telling at a time, without writing down a single word. Travelling bards would wander the trading routes of Greece, reciting the poetry as they roamed. They could hear the melodic rhythm and repeated refrains that are largely imperceptible to our untrained ears, and the exhilarating escapades of the narrative would make the whole thing far easier to remember than you might imagine. The average audience wouldn't know if you'd missed a bit.

If you read the whole thing in Ancient Greek (I've done so to save you a bit of time), you'll discover the most extraordinary mish-mash of dialects across the work. The same words and phrases are sometimes expressed using different regional accents in various parts of the epic. Even more surprising is that some of the passages are written in much older forms of Greek than others. So, what on earth is going on? It seems to point to the fact that *The Odyssey* wasn't actually written by one man called Homer during a lazy summer in a beachside taverna. No single person would have used such an illogical collection of dialects and archaic language mixed together in one poem. Instead, it seems that the roaming bards collected myths and legends as they travelled through both geography and generations, and wove them into the hypnotic narrative that was eventually put into writing.

Regardless of who Homer was – or whether he was at all – the stories attributed to him have been passed down from one person to another for nearly three thousand years. His most iconic myths continue to be told in new ways today, such as the Trojan Horse, the ten-year War of Troy and the brutish Cyclops, which is where we pick up the story now.

ARRIVING AT A STRANGE ISLAND

Odysseus and his fleet of twelve ships have been pounded by storms for nine days. They are depleted in both vessels and men, and have been blown further off course, further still from home. As night falls, they sail cautiously through the misty darkness. Their boats are guided safely by an unseen god, and they are surprised to beach gently on a low, forested island.

When Dawn stretches her rosy fingers across the sky, the mainland is bathed in her glow just across the water. They see an abundant but uncultivated terrain. Zeus' rains have nourished a fertile landscape teeming with wheat, barley and vines, none of which has been ploughed or harvested. There are no signs of a harbour or boats. Whoever lives here cannot be part of a civilized society. This is a lawless place, where each person – or perhaps creature – fends for themselves.

The island they've moored upon is bountiful with goats, and Odysseus' men get hunting. All afternoon and into the evening, each of his ships' crews feasts on nine goats and has quite the party with skinfuls of wine, plundered from cities they have ransacked along their unplanned route.

THE CYCLOPS

Odysseus and his men are so close to the shore of the mainland that they can hear the voices of the Cyclops giants, they can see their smoke and they can hear their sheep and goats bleating. In the morning, Odysseus takes his boat across the water to discover who his unsuspecting hosts might be. Directly on the new shore, stands a vast, gaping cave. That's when they catch their first glimpse of its inhabitant, Polyphemus. This hulking, monstrous creature is as much a colossal mountain as he is a man, his hideous face blinking with one gigantic eye. Around the cave's entrance are arranged towering boulders and mighty pine trees to create a pen for his flocks.

Even in the land of the Cyclops, this giant is an outcast. He lives a lonely life separated from his neighbours, separated from laws and justice, and grazing his sheep far away. Odysseus takes just twelve of his strongest fighters to take a closer look, carrying with them a skin of particularly potent, undiluted red wine. By the time they reach the cave, Polyphemus is away with his flocks. Odysseus' men gasp at what they find inside. A huge array of cheeses is piled high on racks, buckets brim-full with milk, pales full of whey, and three pens of young goats and lambs.

It's not until the end of the day that the mountain-man returns. The ground shudders with each of his steps and, as a thunderous crash reverberates around the cave, he throws down the logs he has gathered during the day. All the male sheep and goats he leaves outside, herding the females inside the vast cavern to milk early the following morning. Odysseus and his men hide in the shadows to observe their host. They are horrified as he lifts a colossal boulder and seals the entrance. Not even twenty-two horse-drawn carts could move that thing! They are trapped. It's not until he lights a fire that Polyphemus sees the small men, who are cautiously pressed into a corner.

'Strangers!' he bellows out. 'Who are you and where are you from?'

His monstrous voice shakes the walls. This is not the hospitable welcome Odysseus and his men were hoping for. Despite the utter terror coursing through him,

Odysseus steels himself to relate the tale of their terrible and hard-fought quest to find their way home. He appeals to the monster to respect Zeus and the gods by offering his guests a warm welcome – this is the custom, after all.

'Stranger,' comes the gut-wrenching reply, 'you must be a fool if you think you can tell me to fear the gods.' Odysseus' heart sinks. 'We Cyclops don't care one bit about Zeus or his anger. We have far more power than he does. If I were to spare you or your men, it would be because I feel like it, not for some fear of the gods.'

At that, the looming ogre grabs two of Odysseus' men in one hand and hammers their heads against the ground like an unthinking toddler. Their brains splatter out across the floor and soak the earth. With a blank look on his beastly face, Polyphemus pulls their limbs off one by one, and sucks their bodies clean like a chicken wing. Finally, he pops the rest in his mouth and crunches down until every last piece of Odysseus' companions is gone. The men collapse to their knees and cry out to Zeus for help, utterly paralysed where they fall. The mighty Cyclops carries on with his evening chores, as Odysseus and his remaining men withdraw to the recesses of the cave in horror.

ODYSSEUS' CUNNING PLAN

The following day doesn't bring much better fortune: Polyphemus milks his flocks in the morning and takes them out all afternoon to pasture, blocking the huge entrance each time he comes or goes. In the evening, he grabs at two more of Odysseus' men and dispatches them as swiftly and gruesomely as before. They must kill the Cyclops. But, with that massive boulder blocking the entrance, how will they ever get out? No – Odysseus must come up with a much shrewder plan.

On the third day, while Polyphemus is out, the men find the giant's club – a huge trunk of olive wood as large as a ship's mast. They cut it in half with the giant's tools and saw a sharp point at one end, struggling to lower it into the embers of the fire to harden the wood. Later that evening, after two more men have been smashed and crunched, Odysseus takes a deep breath and steps forward into the light of the creature's fire. He lifts up a large bowl of the heady red wine they carried with them and offers it to Polyphemus.

'Here, Cyclops, have some of this wine to finish off your meal of human flesh,' he says with confidence in his voice. 'I brought it to you as an offering, hoping that you would show me pity and help me on my way home. But you are unbearable and terrible. The horror of how you treat us!'

A giant hand grabs the bowl of wine and the Cyclops downs the lot. He demands a second bowlful, then a third, and each time drinks every last drop. As his head starts to roll, he asks Odysseus who he is.

'You want to know what they call me? My name is Nobody – that's what everyone knows me as.'

'What a name!' booms the reply. 'Well, my gift of hospitality to you, Nobody, is that I will eat you last of all your men. You're welcome.'

With that, he falls down onto his back and starts to snore noisily with his head fallen to the side. Odysseus gets to work. With four of his remaining men, he carries the huge olive mast to the fire and holds it there until it is glowing hot. With all their strength and as much force as they can muster, they lift it up to the ogre's head and drive it directly through the Cyclops' eye.

His blood sizzles with the heat, and his face burns with black smoke. His eyeball hisses, crackles and bursts as they drive the stake in further. Polyphemus' horrifying roar resonates about the cave and nearly deafens the men. The sound is so terrible that even his neighbouring giants hear his pain. Many of them come rushing to the outside of his shelter to ask who has attacked him.

'Nobody!' comes the call from within the cavern. 'Nobody is using trickery to try and kill me!'

The Cyclops can't believe their ears. Each of them rolls his eye and turns to make his way home again. The oddball is making a huge calamity about nothing. Polyphemus groans and wails with excruciating pain. 'I will get you, Nobody, and your men.'

ESCAPING THE CAVE

Blinded, Polyphemus feels his way through the cave and shifts the vast boulder from the entrance. He sits his huge mass across the opening to block anyone who would try to leave. Odysseus sees just one way that they can escape the giant and find their way out of the cave.

He approaches the Cyclops' flocks – the sheep will provide cover for Odysseus and his men. He straps groups of three sheep side by side, and each of his men attaches himself to the underside of one of the middle creatures.

This way, they are hidden by wool and the busy flock bustling to leave the cave. Polyphemus gropes at each set of sheep as they pass, but does not uncover the daring break for freedom.

ODYSSEUS' BIG MISTAKE

The men bolt for the ship and the crew row with all their strength to escape the land of the Cyclops. But Odysseus is a proud man. He cannot leave without taunting Polyphemus.

'I'm no coward, Cyclops!' he calls back towards the cave. 'Your unspeakable crimes have come back to you. You are a grotesque cannibal, and so Zeus has punished you!'

Hearing the direction of Odysseus' voice, the Cyclops realizes he has been tricked once again by the man. He is so furious at the double-deceit that he lifts off a huge boulder from the rocky cliffs, raises it high above his monstrous head, and hurls it through the air. The gigantic rock flies effortlessly towards Odysseus' ship, and plunges into the dark sea just ahead of them. It sets off a towering tidal wave of water that rushes towards them, nearly submerging the vessel, and drives them in one go back to the beach they have just departed. Once again, they use their full strength to row away from the land of the Cyclops. And once again, Odysseus calls back to taunt the beast. His men plead with him to control his pride, but he will not be convinced.

'Cyclops!' he shouts. 'If anyone asks you who it was that

blinded you, tell them it was Odysseus, plunderer of cities, son of Laertes, and king of Ithaca. That is who gouged out your eye.'

Despite our hero's pride, Polyphemus has the last word. He opens his hands to the heavens and as dark clouds gather, he calls to the god of the sea, Poseidon.

'Poseidon! God of the sea and shaker of the earth. You claim to be my father, and if it is so, see to it that Odysseus – plunderer of cities, son of Laertes, and king of Ithaca – never makes it back to his home.' He doubles down on the curse: 'Or if he does make it to Ithaca, that he does so without a single one of his men or ships intact, and that there he finds his home in utter ruin and turmoil.'

While the story of the Cyclops ends there, his impact has only just begun. Poseidon hears the prayer, and continues to harass Odysseus and his men on their journey home. In the end, our hero is the only one to make it back to Ithaca alive, where he must defeat his wife's suitors. His legendary pride is eventually Odysseus' downfall.

Epilogue:

The Story Continues

any of the myths and legends in this book were invented by our ancient ancestors to help them make sense of the world they observed. Extraordinary gods, creatures and forces became the central characters in fantastic tales that explained the creation of the earth, the passage of the sun, the heartbreak of death and the all-consuming power of love.

Some of the stories you have read are literal translations of inscriptions and scripts made many thousands of years ago. Other stories have been miraculously passed from one person's lips to another person's imagination across countless generations of storytellers for several millennia to reach these pages. The relatability of the heroes' emotions, desires and pain in those tales reveals how little humanity changes across the aeons.

Myths are not just a means to explain the natural world around us. Much like the Trojan Horse, the tales themselves are vessels that hold within them important messages for the society that told them. Stories are a memorable way to communicate how a society should live, why they practise certain customs, and what their place in the history of the world might be. Over time, myths work their way into the cultural identity of the people that are telling them. They are entertaining and unforgettable ways to pass on a huge amount of information across the generations.

The importance of myth as cultural identity is never clearer than in societies whose history has been deliberately oppressed. Enslaved people who were forced from West Africa to the Americas had no possessions and no link to their homeland other than the stories they could tell. The Maya identity and language was outlawed by Spanish colonizers and it only survived in real terms through the legends that were passed down. The ancient myths of the many First Nations across the Australian continent are still rarely committed to writing and continue to live through the retelling from one generation to the next.

The power of stories to unite us, define us and guide us has been an intrinsic part of being human since the dawn of society, and the stories will continue for as long as we have messages to share.

Acknowledgements

I express huge gratitude to the whole team at Michael O'Mara Books in putting this book together. My special thanks go to Gabriella Nemeth for bringing the whole project into fruition; to Nick Fawcett for his thoughtful copy-editing; to Alice Furse for the creative publicity; and to Aubrey Smith for his phenomenal illustrations that capture the oldest stories ever told in a beautiful way.

Index